DAUGHTERS OF EVE

DAUGHTERS OF EVE

Women in the Bible

by Frederick Drimmer
Illustrations by Hal Frenck

The C. R. Gibson Company, Norwalk, Connecticut

CONTENTS

The Power of Faith 9
Hannah—The Shunammite—Priscilla—The Poor Widow
The Woman of Canaan—Mary and Martha—Sapphira

The Proud and the Humble 17
Hagar—The Widow of Zarephath—Michal
Dorcas (Tabitha)—Miram—Salome

The True Believers—and the False 25
Jezebel—Eunice and Lois—Mary Magdalene—Anna
The Woman of Samaria—Phebe—Elisabeth
Jeroboam's Wife—The Woman Who Touched Jesus

The Serving and the Self-Serving 35
Delilah—Samson's Mother—Athaliah
The Witch of Endor—Ruth and Orpah
The Daughters of Zelophehad—Jephthah's Daughter

The Power of Courage 47
Deborah and Jael—Pilate's Wife—Esther and Vashti
Job's Wife—Naomi—Lydia—Rahab
Widow of the Two Mites

Love and Hate 55
Mary, Mother of Jesus—The Two Mothers
Rachel and Leah—Herodias and Salome—Rizpah
The Woman of Timnath

Women of Wisdom, Women of Folly 67
Eve—Abigail—Rebekah—Lot's Wife—Jochebed
The Queen of Sheba—Huldah

The Chaste and the Unchaste 77
Bathsheba—Sarah—The Sinful Woman—Potiphar's Wife
Dinah—Gomer—Tamar

The Scriptures are filled with interesting stories, but none are more fascinating than those which tell about the women in the Bible.

Some were weak, some were strong; some wise and some foolish, but all were women of purpose who could perform great deeds or could quietly find ways to change the course of history.

Beginning with Eve, and with each of the Daughters of Eve *we are treated to a wealth of personal experience that offers insight and understanding for today.*

We discover the wonder of the feminine mystique operating at all levels of activity to influence and often to control the powerful forces of life. We learn about the pitiful fruits of folly, the true rewards of virtue. We see how adversity can result from a love of power, and how glorious can be the power of love.

And overall, there is the everlasting presence of God turning an omnipotent face from those who stray, yet ready to forgive and help all who have faith and seek him.

Times have changed but truth is constant, and in Daughters of Eve *the lives of the women in the Bible provide examples of the human spirt searching for fulfilment.*

— The Editors

The Power of Faith

And Jesus answering saith unto them, Have faith in God. For verily I say unto you, That whosoever shall say unto this mountain, Be thou removed, and be thou cast into the sea; and shall not doubt in his heart, but shall believe that those things which he saith shall come to pass; he shall have whatsoever he saith.

— Mark 11:22-23

Faith can work miracles. We see it in a thousand ways.

No woman can achieve as much as the woman who has faith in God. Faith brings renewed life, nourishes the hungry, and heals the afflicted. Mary and Martha had faith in God and He raised their brother, Lazarus, from the dead. Hannah was barren for years, but because she had faith she was able to bear a son, the prophet Samuel. Many other miracles have been worked by people with great faith.

Faith unleashes tremendous reserves of strength and endurance. Without it we become fragile reeds, unprotected from the ravaging winds.

Hannah I SAMUEL 1:2-28, 2:19-21

The name Hannah means "grace or compassion". God was gracious to Hannah, for her faith was boundless. God heard her prayers because she put her whole heart into them.

Hannah was a wife of Elkanah, who lived on Mount Ephraim. Although her husband loved her, the Lord had made her childless, and it grieved her.

"Am not I better to thee than ten sons?" Hannah's husband asked, seeking to comfort her. But she went on grieving.

For all her sorrow, Hannah never forgot to pray to the Lord. One day she had gone up to Shiloh, where Eli was priest. He sat before the temple and after a while he noticed her. Others were bowed in prayer, and Eli could hear their fervent voices. Hannah's prayers, however, he could not hear, although he could

9

see her lips moving. He decided she must be drunk, and he became angry for she was before the house of the Lord.

"Put away thy wine from thee," he ordered her reproachfully.

"I have drunk neither wine nor strong drink," Hannah answered humbly, "but have poured out my soul before the Lord."

The priest could see she was speaking the truth. "The God of Israel grant thee thy petition that thou hast asked of him," he said.

A peace descended upon Hannah, a peace such as she had not known. Not long afterward she conceived, and she bore a son whom she named Samuel.

After the boy was weaned, Hannah brought him to Eli in the temple. "For this child I prayed," she said, "and the Lord hath given me my petition which I asked of him. Therefore I have lent him to the Lord."

Eli accepted the boy and raised him to be a priest. Every year Hannah came with her husband to the temple to offer sacrifice and to see her son, and each time she brought him a new coat she had made.

The Lord blessed this loving mother and she bore five more children. But none meant more to her than Samuel, the child of her prayers. Samuel became one of the great Hebrew prophets, and under his vigorous leadership, kept his country strong in the faith.

The Shunammite II KINGS 4:8-37

God's miracles surpass human understanding and for the Lord all things are possible.

In Shunem of old Palestine, there lived a wealthy woman. From time to time the prophet Elisha passed her house and she offered him food. It was considered a blessing to do anything for a holy man. This pious woman had a room built on to her house, where she invited the prophet to stay whenever he visited Shunem.

Elisha was grateful to the Shunammite woman for her unfailing hospitality. When he learned she had no child and her husband was old, he prophesied that she would conceive and bear a son.

The Shunammite had faith, and it happened to her as the prophet had foretold. The boy grew and was well, but one fateful day, when he was in the fields with his father, he fell to the ground, crying, "My head, my head!" He was carried home and died in his mother's arms.

In her grief, the Shunammite thought of the holy man.

"It shall be well," she said to her husband, and she rode off to Carmel, where Elisha dwelled.

Elisha saw the woman coming. "Run now, I pray thee," he said to his servant, "and say unto her, Is it well with thee? is it well with thy husband? is it well with the child?" We know why the Shunammite was coming to the prophet, but her reply to the servant was, "It is well."

The woman's face told the prophet more than her words, and he went to her house, where the child had been placed upon Elisha's bed. Elisha lay upon him and put his mouth to the boy's mouth. The child's flesh became warm again. He sneezed and opened his eyes.

"Take up thy son," said Elisha to the woman.

Bowing to the ground, the woman gave thanks to the Lord and this holy man.

Priscilla ACTS 18:2, 18, 26; ROMANS 16:3-4; I CORINTHIANS 16:19; II TIMOTHY 4:19

Priscilla, with her husband, Aquila, a Jew, had much in common with Saint Paul. Like him, they were tentmakers. Like him, they believed in the true God at a time when there were few followers. When Paul came to Corinth, where they lived, he stayed with them, and they worked at their craft together and preached the word of the Lord. They also traveled with him as fellow missionaries when he went to Syria.

Priscilla and her husband opened their home to their fellow Christians as a place of prayer in the perilous days when the new

11

faith was taking its first steps in Europe. In Ephesus they won to Christ a powerful convert, Apollos, a great teacher of the Scriptures.

Paul valued Priscilla and Aquila as friends and disciples. "Greet Priscilla and Aquila my helpers in Christ Jesus," he said in his Epistle to the Romans, "who have for my life laid down their own necks: unto whom not only I give thanks, but also all the churches of the Gentiles."

The Poor Widow II KINGS 4:1-7

Elisha did the Lord's work in a way that often foreshadowed the miracles of Jesus. One day a distressed widow turned to the prophet for aid: she was deeply in debt and a creditor had come to take her two sons as slaves in payment.

Elisha was moved. "Tell me, what hast thou in the house?" he asked the poor woman.

"Thine handmaid hath not any thing in the house," said she, "save a pot of oil."

Elisha told her to borrow as many vessels as she could from her neighbors. Then he instructed her to pour oil into them from her pot.

The obedient widow followed the prophet's order. She poured and poured from the one pot and miraculously was able to fill the multitude of vessels.

"Go, sell the oil, and pay thy debt," the man of God said to her, "and live thou and thy children of the rest."

The Woman of Canaan MATTHEW 15:21-28

12

The mercy of the Son of God is infinite. The Holy Book bears witness to His unfailing willingness to answer the prayers of those who have faith in Him.

Once, when Jesus was traveling along the coasts of Tyre and Sidon, a woman of Canaan came to Him.

"Have mercy on me, O Lord, thou son of David," she said. "My daughter is grievously vexed with a devil."

Jesus had much work and little time. He reminded the woman that His mission was to the children of Israel. "It is not meet to take the children's bread, and to cast it to the dogs."

But the woman, being so close to the source of all help, would not give up. "The dogs eat of the crumbs which fall form their masters' table," she said.

The woman's humility and her faith in him touched the Lord. "O woman, great is thy faith," He replied. "Be it unto thee even as thou wilt."

And that same hour the woman's daughter was freed of her affliction.

Mary and Martha LUKE 10:38-42; JOHN 11:1-45; 12:2-8

No one was more devoted to Jesus than Mary and her sister Martha. Their brother, Lazarus, was also a good friend of the Lord. Mary, Martha, and Lazarus lived in Bethany, and whenever Jesus came that way they gave Him a warm welcome.

The two sisters present fascinatingly different portraits in character. Martha had the characteristics we often see in women prominent in the church. She was a doer, energetic, resourceful, tireless, born to command. Although she concerned herself mostly with the matter-of-fact things of this world, she was also a deeply religious person, dedicated to the teachings of the Lord. Harriet Beecher Stowe has characterized Martha and women like her in these words: "They manage fairs, they dress churches, they get up religious festivals, their names are on committees, they are known at celebrations, they rule their own homes with activity and diligence, and they are justly honored by all who know them . . . Jesus loved Martha. He understood her, He appreciated her worth, and He loved her."

13

Mary was just as dear to Jesus as her sister. She was warm-hearted, generous, and impulsive. In contrast to Martha, she seems to have been less involved with material things. Religion could fill her mind and her heart, so she might forget all about the practical demands of daily life.

The Bible gives us some memorable pictures of the two sisters. At one time Jesus and His followers came to their house. The family welcomed them in and He began to teach. Mary (perhaps she was the younger sister) sat at His feet in rapture, drinking in every word. Martha, meanwhile, bustled about, serving refreshments to the crowd. Perhaps she asked Mary to help her, but Mary was so interested in the Lord's teachings that she didn't hear. Finally Martha became very annoyed. She went up to Jesus.

"Lord," said Martha, "dost thou not care that my sister hath left me to serve alone? bid her therefore that she help me."

Jesus's reply is typical of His unique way of dealing with people. It expressed sympathy for Martha almost as much as it did rebuke. "Martha, Martha," He said, "thou art careful and troubled about many things: But one thing is needful: and Mary hath chosen that good part, which shall not be taken away from her."

Another time Lazarus, brother of Mary and Martha, became sick, and the sisters summoned Jesus to help. But Jesus tarried, and their brother died. Mary, in her grief, told the Lord that if He had been there her brother would not have died. And Jesus, for the first time, spoke these great words of hope and promise:

"I am the resurrection and the life: he that believeth in me, though he were dead, yet shall he live."

Lazarus had been dead for four days, but when Jesus called to him he came out of his tomb and was alive and well again.

Six days before the Last Supper Jesus came to their house again. The family prepared a meal and Martha served it. Then Mary took a pound of costly ointment, anointed the Lord's feet with it, and wiped them with her hair. When Judas grumbled that the oil could have been sold and the money given to the poor, Jesus rebuked him. "Let her alone: against the day of my burying hath she kept this. For the poor always ye have with you; but me ye have not always."

By their deep love and faith, Mary and Martha earned a shining place in the greatest story ever told.

Sapphira ACTS 5:1-10

Sapphira was an early Christian, but like her husband, Ananias, she only half believed. Their lack of faith led them to imagine they could deceive the Lord.

It was the custom that disciples of Christ who were well-to-do should sell their possessions and give the money they received to the apostles to distribute to those in need. Ananias and Sapphira sold their land but Ananias only gave a part of the price, saying it was all he had received. He meant to keep the rest for himself.

"Why hath Satan filled thine heart to lie to the Holy Ghost, and to keep back part of the price of the land?" Peter asked Ananias. Transfixed with guilt, Ananias fell dead at the holy man's feet.

Three hours later Ananias's wife came in. Peter asked how much she and her husband had sold the land for and she told the same lie her husband had.

"How is it," Peter asked her, "that ye have agreed to tempt together the Spirit of the Lord? behold, the feet of them which have buried thy husband are at the door, and shall carry thee out."

Retribution came to Sapphira as swiftly as it had to her husband, for the Lord can punish as well as reward.

15

The Proud and the Humble

For whosoever exalteth himself shall be abased; and he that humbleth himself shall be exalted.

— Luke 14:11

Of all the things the Bible teaches, one of the greatest lessons is that one should never give up hope. God will preserve the meek. The Bible shows us again and again that the Lord delights in raising up those who falter and fall—and He smites those who become overproud. No one was more humble and meek than His Son, Jesus Christ. No one was humiliated more. And no one was raised to greater glory.

It is a mistake to envy the proud and the mighty, the rich, the successful. The Bible tells of many great ones who were unhappy. Some of them had magnificent opportunities, but through pride they destroyed them. Miriam, sister of Moses, became overconfident of her powers, and the Lord punished her terribly. Queen Michal looked down upon her husband because of the way he showed his love for God, and she paid a heavy price. Salome was so proud of her sons, James and John, that she thought they deserved a special place in heaven, but Jesus rebuked her.

It is God's way to humble the proud. It is also His way to lift up the humble. In God's kingdom, . . . "Many that are first shall be last; and the last shall be first" Matthew 19:30.

Hagar   GENESIS 16:1-16

Humble people can be chosen to fill high places. But they must prove worthy of those places and not allow vanity to turn their heads the way a foolish girl named Hagar did.

Hagar was a young Egyptian, handmaid to Sarah (Sarai). Sarah's marriage to the patriarch Abraham (Abram) had not been blessed with children. Gravely troubled, she proposed to her husband that he take her handmaid to wife. Such was the custom in Old Testament times when a woman proved barren.

Abraham agreed.

In a short time Hagar became pregnant. As her waist thickened, her vanity grew. After all, she told herself—and, no doubt, anyone else who would listen—she had succeeded where her mistress had failed. Forgetting she was still Sarah's servant, she began to treat her with contempt.

Insult had been added to injury, and Sarah could not stand it for long. Although Hagar was carrying Abraham's child, she had not taken Sarah's place in his heart. "Behold, thy maid is in thy hand," he told Sarah when she complained about Hagar's misconduct. "Do to her as it pleaseth thee."

Sarah dealt harshly with Hagar—so harshly that the handmaid ran away. Later she returned. But neither Hagar nor the son she bore, Ishmael, could ever cleanse themselves of the sin of pride. In the end, to keep the peace, Abraham had to send the two away for good.

The Widow of Zarephath I KINGS 17:9-24

In a time of drought and famine, the Lord spoke to the prophet Elijah. "Arise, get thee to Zarephath, which belongeth to Zidon, and dwell there: behold, I have commanded a widow woman there to sustain thee."

When the prophet came to the gate of the city, he saw the woman. She was the poorest of the poor. He asked her to bring him a drink of water and a morsel of bread.

The water she was ready to bring, but the bread . . . "As the Lord thy God liveth," she said, "I have not a cake, but an handful of meal in a barrel, and a little oil in a cruse: and, behold, I am gathering two sticks, that I may go in and dress it for me and my son, that we may eat it, and die."

Elijah told her not to worry, but to make him a little cake first. "For thus saith the Lord God of Israel, The barrel of meal shall no waste, neither shall the cruse of oil fail, until the day that the Lord sendeth rain upon the earth."

The Lord had chosen the poor woman wisely. She made the

cake for Elijah without worrying about what she and her son would have to eat. And God's words were fulfilled. To the woman's enormous surprise, whenever she went to her barrel or her cruse, she found all the meal and oil she needed. Whatever she took was miraculously replaced.

But this was not the only blessing God bestowed on the humble widow for her goodness to Elijah. Later her son became sick and he died. The unhappy woman thought it was a punishment for her sins. But Elijah prayed to God for mercy and the child revived.

The prophet brought the boy to his mother. "See, thy son liveth."

The widow could hardly believe what she saw. "Now by this I know that thou art a man of God, and that the word of the Lord in thy mouth is truth," she told Elijah.

Michal
I SAMUEL 14:49; 18:17-28; 19:11-17; 25:44;
II SAMUEL 3:13-16; 6:16-21

Michal, daughter of King Saul, loved David with all her heart. To save his life, she helped him to escape just before messengers sent by her father came to seize him. Yet in the end, pride made her treat him with scorn, so that his love for her turned to hatred.

The struggle between David and the mad king Saul was a deadly one. Saul knew David had been chosen to replace him on the throne of Israel, and he had made up his mind that, by hook or by crook, he would see David dead first. He offered to give his daughter, Michal, to David on condition that he go out and kill a hundred of the Philistines, the Jews' old enemies. Secretly, he hoped that the young warrior would lose his life in the attempt. But David was a mighty fighter. He returned safe and sound, bringing trophies to show he and his men had slain not one hundred, but two hundred of the enemy. And so the poor shepherd boy suddenly found himself married to a princess, and the son-in-law of a king. It was a happy moment for him. But not for the king.

Saul was as determined as ever to destroy David. He sent assassins to the young man's house to watch and slay him in the

19

morning. Finding out in time, Michal let her husband down through a window. Then she took a statue, put it in David's bed, and covered it up.

Saul's hirelings came in. "He is sick," she said. In only a short while her father discovered the ruse. "Why hast thou deceived me so," he asked, "and sent away mine enemy, that he is escaped?" But Michal insisted that David had substituted the statue himself and threatened to kill her if she gave him away.

David had fled to the wilderness, and there he lived as an outlaw. Her mad father gave Michal to another man, Phalti. Later Phalti was obliged to give her back to her first husband, and he followed her, weeping. To him, as to David, she must have been a fine wife.

When David became king he brought the ark of the Lord into Jerusalem. Overcome with delight, he danced before the ark. Michal looked out of the palace window. She saw her husband leaping and dancing in what seemed to her a most unkingly way, and she despised him in her heart. David, she felt, was behaving like the son of shepherds that he was.

"How glorious was the king of Israel to day," she told him later, her voice dripping sarcasm, "who uncovered himself to day in the eyes of the handmaids of his servants, as one of the vain fellows shamelessly uncovereth himself!"

David was notorious for his quick temper. His wife, better than anyone else, should have known how he would react, but her sense of injured dignity must have blinded her.

"It was before the Lord," David thundered, "which chose me before thy father, and before all his house, to appoint me ruler over the people of the Lord, over Israel: therefore will I play before the Lord."

For her pride, Michal was humbled. David refused to have anything more to do with her. Sitting alone, without a husband, condemned never to have children, she must have regretted more than once that she had placed her pride of rank before her love for King David.

Dorcas (TABITHA) ACTS 9:36-42

God performs miracles for the faithful and the humble. He performed a very great one for Dorcas.

Dorcas was a Christian disciple who lived in Joppa (today's Jaffa, on the Israel coast). She was revered for her good works, and she gave alms whenever she could. Humble in word and deed, she labored with her needle constantly, making clothing which she gave to those who needed it. The faithful called her Tabitha, her name in Aramaic.

One day Dorcas became sick and to the dismay of the Christian congregation, she died. The disciples sent for Peter, who was at nearby Lydda. When he came, they took him to the upper chamber, where Dorcas was laid out for burial. The women, weeping, showed the apostle the coats and other garments she had made for them.

Peter's heart went out to Dorcas. He sent everyone from the room and he knelt down and prayed. Then he turned to the body and said, "Tabitha, arise."

The dead woman stirred. She opened her eyes and sat up.

Taking her by the hand, Peter presented her, living, to the astonished mourners.

Miriam EXODUS 15:20-21; NUMBERS 12:1-16; 20:1; 26:59; DEUTERONOMY 24:9; MICAH 6:4

Miriam was the sister of Israel's great leader, Moses. It was she who kept watch over her baby brother when his little ark floated among the bulrushes in the Nile. It was she who told Pharaoh's daughter to hire a nurse—the baby's own mother—to take care of Moses.

Miriam had been chosen by God for great things. The Lord even made her a prophetess and spoke to her in visions, but it was not enough for her. She wanted to take Moses's place with the Lord.

Like Moses and her other brother, Aaron, Miriam was a leader. After Moses had brought the children of Israel through the Red Sea, she danced a dance of triumph, and the women followed her. Taking a timbrel in her hand, she called them to raise up their voices. "Sing ye to the Lord, for he hath triumphed gloriously; for the horse and his rider hath he thrown into the sea."

She must have been a woman with a strong personality and a bold voice. By contrast, her brother Moses, the Book of Numbers tells us, was a meek man. She felt she and Aaron had as much right to lead as Moses did, since she and Aaron both heard the Lord's voice in visions and in dreams. When Moses offended his brother and sister by marrying a woman of another race, they talked against him. "Hath the Lord indeed spoken only by Moses?" they said. "Hath he not also spoken by us?"

So Moses faced a rebellion, headed by those who were, or should have been, closest to him. More likely than not, Miriam prompted the revolt, to judge by what happened to her.

When the Lord heard the claims of Miriam and Aaron He was not pleased. "Come out ye three unto the tabernacle of the congregation," He told them and Moses.

At the tabernacle the Lord came down in a pillar of cloud. To Miriam and Aaron He proclaimed that Moses was His chosen instrument. He did not communicate with him just in visions, as He did with them and other prophets. "With him I will speak mouth to mouth," said the Lord.

Now the full measure of God's wrath fell on Miriam. As the pillar of cloud rose from the tabernacle, Aaron saw that his sister's skin had turned white as snow. She had leprosy.

It was a terrible sight, and Aaron was frightened. He turned to Moses. "I beseech thee, lay not the sin upon us, wherein we have done foolishly, and wherein we have sinned."

Moses, the meek one, forgave them readily. He knew where to turn for aid for his stricken sister. "Heal her now, O God, I beseech thee," he prayed.

The Lord heard Moses, but He was still angry with Miriam. He ordered that she be put outside the camp of the Jews for seven days. When she was brought in again, she was whole. The Bible does not mention that she ever spoke out against her brother again.

Miriam, like Moses and Aaron, did not live to see the Promised Land. She died while the children of Israel were staying in Kadesh and she was buried there.

Salome MATTHEW 20:20-28

To Jesus, one day, came Salome, mother of his disciples James and John. Salome was a holy woman and a faithful one, but she was a mother, and like many a mother she was overproud of her sons.

"Grant," said Salome to Jesus, "that these my two sons may sit, the one on thy right hand, and the other on the left, in thy kingdom."

"To sit on my right hand, and on my left," Jesus admonished her, "is not mine to give, but it shall be given to them for whom it is prepared of my Father."

The places that Salome asked, Jesus said, had to be earned. "He that will be chief among you, let him be your servant."

Salome accepted the rebuke with a good grace. A loving follower of the Lord, she was at the foot of the cross when He died on Calvary.

23

The True Believers—
and the False

. . . They called on the name of Baal from morning even until noon, saying, O Baal, hear us. But there was no voice, nor any that answered.

—I Kings 18:26.

"Ye shall know the truth," said Jesus, "and the truth shall make you free." But many times it seems as if people do not want to know the truth and do not want to be free. They prefer to go through life in chains, often of their own making.

Although the Lord made Himself manifest to the children of Israel in ancient times, they frequently wavered in their faith. When Moses tarried on Mount Sinai his people became impatient and made themselves a calf of gold to worship. When Jezebel and Ahab set up Baal and other idols, the people bowed down to them. But the worship of idols brought the Israelites nothing but disappointment and despair.

In the Bible were many who destroyed themselves because they followed false gods. Only those who were true believers found salvation. Like the humble woman of Samaria, whom Jesus asked for a drink—and to whom He then gave the water of eternal life. And Elisabeth, who had such faith thatGod granted her dearest wish. And Mary Magdalene, who followed the Master to the tomb and beyond. And other women who also chose the right path—who laid up for themselves "treasures in heaven, where neither moth nor rust doth corrupt, and where thieves do not break through or steal" (Matthew 6:20).

25

Jezebel I KINGS 16:31-33; 18:4, 13, 19-39; 19:1-8; 21:1-29;
II KINGS 9:7, 10, 22, 30-37

The name Jezebel has come to symbolize the shameless and abandoned woman. She was a worshiper of idols and a servant to the god Baal. Her story is a warning to anyone tempted to follow in her ways.

Jezebel who lived in the ninth century B.C., was a daughter of the king of Sidon, a great seaport in ancient Phoenicia. She would have been lost to memory long ages ago if she had not married a king of Israel, Ahab. To his palace in Samaria she brought her idols. She also brought a small army of heathen priests. Ahab joined his wife in worshiping Baal, and he gave her a free hand in matters of religion.

Like her gods, Jezebel demanded human sacrifice. Looking upon Jehovah as her enemy, she began a campaign of extermination against his priests. Without the help of the great prophet Elijah, every last one of them would have been slain.

In his long war against Queen Jezebel and her idols, Elijah had no weapon but his faith. He never doubted in his victory when he challenged the priests of Baal to a contest that would show which was the true god—Baal or Jehovah.

The scene of the contest was Mount Carmel. Elijah and his supporters and the idol worshipers met there, and each side prepared a bullock for sacrifice. Then Jezebel's priests called on their god to show his power by setting fire to the bullock they had killed. They prayed and prayed, but nothing happened.

Elijah's turn came next. He raised his eyes and his voice to the Lord. Suddenly fire fell from heaven and the bullock was burned to ashes. As a signal from Elijah his supporters seized the priests of Baal and slew them.

Jezebel could not control her rage when she learned that Elijah had killed her priests. "So let the gods do to me, and more also," she told the prophet in a message, "if I make not thy life as the life of one of them by to morrow about this time." Elijah had to flee at once. Unopposed, Jezebel continued as powerful as ever.

Throughout her realm the queen did whatever she wanted without fear of God or man. Once her husband coveted the vineyard of Naboth, which stood next to his palace. When Naboth refused to sell it, Ahab was so unhappy he lost interest in eating.

"Dost thou now govern the kingdom of Israel?" Jezebel asked her husband. "Arise, and eat bread, and let thine heart be merry: I will give thee the vineyard of Naboth."

Now Jezebel set a sinister plan in motion. She ordered a public fast to be proclaimed. Naboth was set on high, and two of her henchmen stood up to accuse him of blaspheming God and the king. The people, their passions aroused, stoned the innocent man. So his garden passed into the king's hands.

The list of Ahab's and Jezebel's crimes was growing longer and longer. Finally God ordered a new king, Jehu, to be anointed in Ahab's place. "The dogs shall eat Jezebel," the Lord said, "and there shall be none to bury her." To the sound of trumpets, Jehu set out to destroy the house of Ahab.

As Jehu rode toward the royal palace, Jezebel prepared to receive him. She painted her face and had her hair dressed. Then she put her head out of the window and shouted a sharp-tongued reproach at the new king.

Jehu glanced up. "Who is on my side?" he called. Two or three eunuchs looked out. "Throw her down!" he cried.

As Jezebel's body struck the pavement her blood spattered the wall. Contemptuously, Jehu rode over her. When he decided to have her buried, the Book of Kings says, "they found no more of her than the skull, and the feet, and the palms of her hands."

Eunice and Lois ACTS 16:1; II TIMOTHY 1:5

Eunice and Lois were the mother and grandmother of Timothy, to whom Paul wrote two of his Epistles. "My dearly beloved son," Paul called him.

It was from these two holy ladies that Timothy learned holiness. In a time when it was dangerous to be a Christian they dared to be followers of Jesus. Paul, writing to Timothy, refers to the "unfeigned faith" that is in him, "which dwelt first in thy grandmother Lois, and thy mother Eunice."

Eunice, we know, was a Jewess who had been converted. Her faith was an intrinsic part of her life and she communicated it to her son, Timothy. He became a close friend and companion of Paul, who sent him on missions to the churches in Thessalonika and Corinth.

Timothy became the first bishop of Ephesus and was a friend of the apostle John. During the reign of the emperor Nero, he was martyred for his faith.

Mary Magdalene
MATTHEW 27:56, 61; 28:1; MARK 15:40, 47; 16:1, 9; LUKE 8:2; 24:10; JOHN 19:25; 20:1, 11-18

Jezebel, and now Mary Magdalene: what a world of difference there was between the two! Jezebel was darkness; Mary was pure light. Jezebel was cruelty; Mary was tenderness and love.

Mary believed in the power of Jesus, for she had felt it in her own person. She was called Magdalene because she came from the town of Magdala (the modern el-Mejdel, a few miles from Tiberias). It was probably on one of His visits there that Jesus first encountered her. Mary was possessed of seven devils and Jesus cast them out of her. This may actually have been on different occasions. Some scholars say the devils were really a nervous disease of which Jesus cured Mary.

Mary (or Miriam) was a popular name in old Palestine. It was the name of Jesus's own mother. It was the name of Lazarus's sister, who listened intently at the Master's feet. Wherever Jesus went, there were Marys to serve him. Few could have loved Him more than Mary Magdalene. If she won special glory by being the first to see the Master after the Resurrection, certainly she won it by her faithful service and ministrations.

28

After Jesus had died on the cross and been laid in the sepulchre, Mary returned on the first day of the week. She found the stone that closed the tomb had been rolled back. Mary wept, fearing the body had been stolen. Then she stooped down to look inside the tomb. Two angels sat where the body had lain. Still weeping, she turned away. Someone was near; she thought it was the gardener. Then that well-known, beloved voice said to her, "Mary." "Rabboni (Master)," she answered, struck with awe.

"Go to my brethren," Jesus told her, "and say unto them, I ascend unto my Father, and your Father; and to my God, and your God."

Mary had now the most wondrous news in the world, and she rushed off to share it with the disciples.

At this point we lose sight of Mary Magdalene. But we cannot doubt that she continued strong in the new faith to the end of her days, serving the Lord and helping to spread the Gospel.

The name of this holy lady has suffered a strange and unfortunate fate. Readers of the Bible confused her with another person, the nameless woman who anointed the Lord's feet in Simon's house (Luke 7:37). That woman had been a sinner. As a result of this misunderstanding, the name Magdalene became a synonym for a reformed prostitute. But the real Mary Magdalene had nothing in her life to be sorry for. She was a saint, not a sinner.

Anna LUKE 2:36-38

Anna had become a widow at a young age and she dedicated the remainder of her life to serving God. The holy temple became her home and she spent her time fasting and praying night and day.

In accordance with the ancient custom, Mary and Joseph brought Jesus to the Temple in Jerusalem to present Him to the Lord and to offer a sacrifice. It was at this time that Simeon, a devout man inspired by the Holy Ghost, took the Child in his arms and thanked the Lord for allowing him to see the Saviour. As Simeon was blessing the Child, Anna entered the chamber and likewise prophesied that Jesus would be the redemption of Israel.

The Woman of Samaria JOHN 4:3-41

How marvelous it must have been to meet Jesus face to face and hear Him speak! That was the blessing of the woman of Samaria. Not only as she converted to faith in His teaching, but she brought many of her countrymen to Him.

"The woman at the well," she is sometimes called. The Lord met her after He had left Judea and was on His way back to Galilee. Passing through Samaria with His disciples, He stopped at a town called Sychar. Jesus was weary, and He sat on a well and rested while His disciples went into town to buy food. It was then that the woman approached with a waterpot.

"Give me to drink," Jesus said.

The woman was astonished. A Jew speaking to her! The children of Israel disliked the Samaritans, who had settled in their land long ago, when they were exiled. Jews had no dealings with Samaritans.

"Whosoever drinketh of this water shall thirst again," "Jesus told her. "But whosoever drinketh of the water that I shall give him shall never thirst; but the water that I shall give him shall be in him a well of water springing up into everlasting life."

Although the Master had never seen the woman before, He told her about her past. "Thou hast had five husbands; and he whom thou now hast is not thy husband."

"Sir, I perceive that thou art a prophet," she said in astonishment.

Jesus spoke on, telling her of His mission to win man to God. The incredible things she was hearing filled her with excitement. Leaving her waterpot, she went into the town.

"Come," she cried to those she met. "See a man, which told me all things that ever I did: is not this the Christ?"

The people who heard her left their tasks and hurried to Jesus. So many came that He tarried in Sychar two days to win them to the truth.

Thus the Master used the humblest of instruments—a sinner—to help Him bring his message to the multitude.

Phebe ROMANS 16:1-2

Of Phebe we know very little, but that little is enough to assure us that she was a good woman and a holy one, for the apostle Paul commended her to the Christians of Rome. She was a helper or a deaconess in the church at Cenchrea, east of Corinth, on the Saronic Gulf in Greece.

In his Epistle to the Romans Paul asked the Christians of Rome to welcome Phebe and to help her in whatever business she had there. He called her "our sister," an expression that tells us how close the members of the early Christian communities felt about each other. "She hath been a succourer of many," he said, "and of myself also." She had helped the Christians of Cenchrea when they were in trouble, and even the apostle himself was indebted to her for her aid.

Paul had infinite confidence in Phebe and it is very likely that he entrusted his Epistle into her hands for delivery to the church of Rome.

Elisabeth LUKE 1:5-80

Elisabeth was a holy woman who led a blameless life. Her one, secret grief was that she was childless. Many times, as the years passed, her heart must have grown heavy when she visited her neighbors and played with their children. Her own house was so silent. The only other person in it was her husband, Zacharias, a priest. He, too, would have dearly loved to have a child.

Faith and goodness can bring miraculous rewards. One day Zacharias was burning incense at the altar in the temple when he looked up and saw an angel before him. The old priest was shaken.

"Fear not, Zacharias," the angel comforted, "for thy prayer is heard; and thy wife Elisabeth shall bear thee a son, and thou shalt call his name John."

The angel foretold that John would be great in the sight of the Lord. Zacharias, listening, shook his head. It was all too hard to believe! But the archangel Gabriel, for it was he himself, declared that Zacharias, because of his disbelief, would be unable to speak until after the child was born.

Perhaps Zacharias began to believe when he came forth from the temple. He was speechless, and speechless he remained. Soon

31

afterward Elisabeth conceived. "For with God," as the angel had said, "nothing shall be impossible."

Elisabeth had a cousin who also conceived six months later. Her name was Mary, and the baby she was to bear would be Jesus. The archangel Gabriel visited Mary, too, and she went to tell Elisabeth about it. Mary stayed with Elisabeth for three months and then went home.

When Elisabeth's full time was come she brought forth a son. On the day of the boy's circumcision Zacharias suddenly found he could speak again. The Holy Ghost filled the old man's spirit and he prophesied: "Thou, child, shalt be called the prophet of the Highest: for thou shalt go before the face of the Lord to prepare his ways."

The child, John, when he became a man, was known as John the Baptist.

Jeroboam's Wife I KINGS 14:1-18

Again and again the children of Israel forsook the true God and bowed down before graven images. During the reign of King Jeroboam in particular—he lived about nine hundred years before Jesus—many turned their backs on Jehovah.

Jeroboam had led a revolt against Rehoboam, Solomon's son, and established the northern kingdom of Israel. Because he wanted to cut his country off utterly from the rest of the Jews he gave his people different gods: two calves of gold, which he set up in Bethel and Dan. In the sight of the Lord this was a monstrous thing.

32   It was not surprising, then, that Jeroboam's son fell sick. His father was deeply worried about him, but he knew better than to pray to false gods for the boy's recovery. In Shiloh there dwelt a prophet of the Lord named Ahijah. Jeroboam told his wife to disguise herself so no one would recognize her and to go to the holy man and ask his help.

As it turned out, the woman's effort to conceal her identity was for nothing. Ahijah was very old and he could no longer see, but he stood close to the Lord. "Behold, the wife of Jeroboam cometh to ask a thing of thee for her son," Jehovah told the blind holy man.

When Ahijah heard the sound of the woman's steps he called out, "Come in, thou wife of Jeroboam; why feignest thou to be another? for I am sent to thee with heavy tidings."

God's words, related by the prophet, were like the cry of her own conscience. Jeroboam's house was to be cast down, for the molten images he had made had provoked the Lord to wrath. Neither would her sick son escape the sins of his father. "When thy feet enter into the city," said Ahijah, "the child shall die."

Fears and regrets must have tormented Jeroboam's wife as she journeyed homeward. Her husband, she knew, would have to pay heavily for his sins, and his sufferings would be her sufferings. And she must have mourned for the child that was doomed to die.

The Woman Who Touched Jesus LUKE 8:43-48

Where doctors are unable to help, true belief may triumph.

There was a woman who suffered from an issue of blood. For twelve years she went from physician to physician, giving them all that she earned, in the hope that they would cure her. No one could help.

The afflicted woman heard that the Physician of Physicians was coming to her town. She worked her way through the crowd that always followed Him. Shyly she touched the hem of His garment.

At once the blood stopped flowing.

"Somebody hath touched me," Jesus said.

33

The woman came forward trembling. She fell at the Master's feet. Her story tumbled from her pale lips.

"Daughter, be of good comfort," Jesus said "Thy faith hath made thee whole; go in peace."

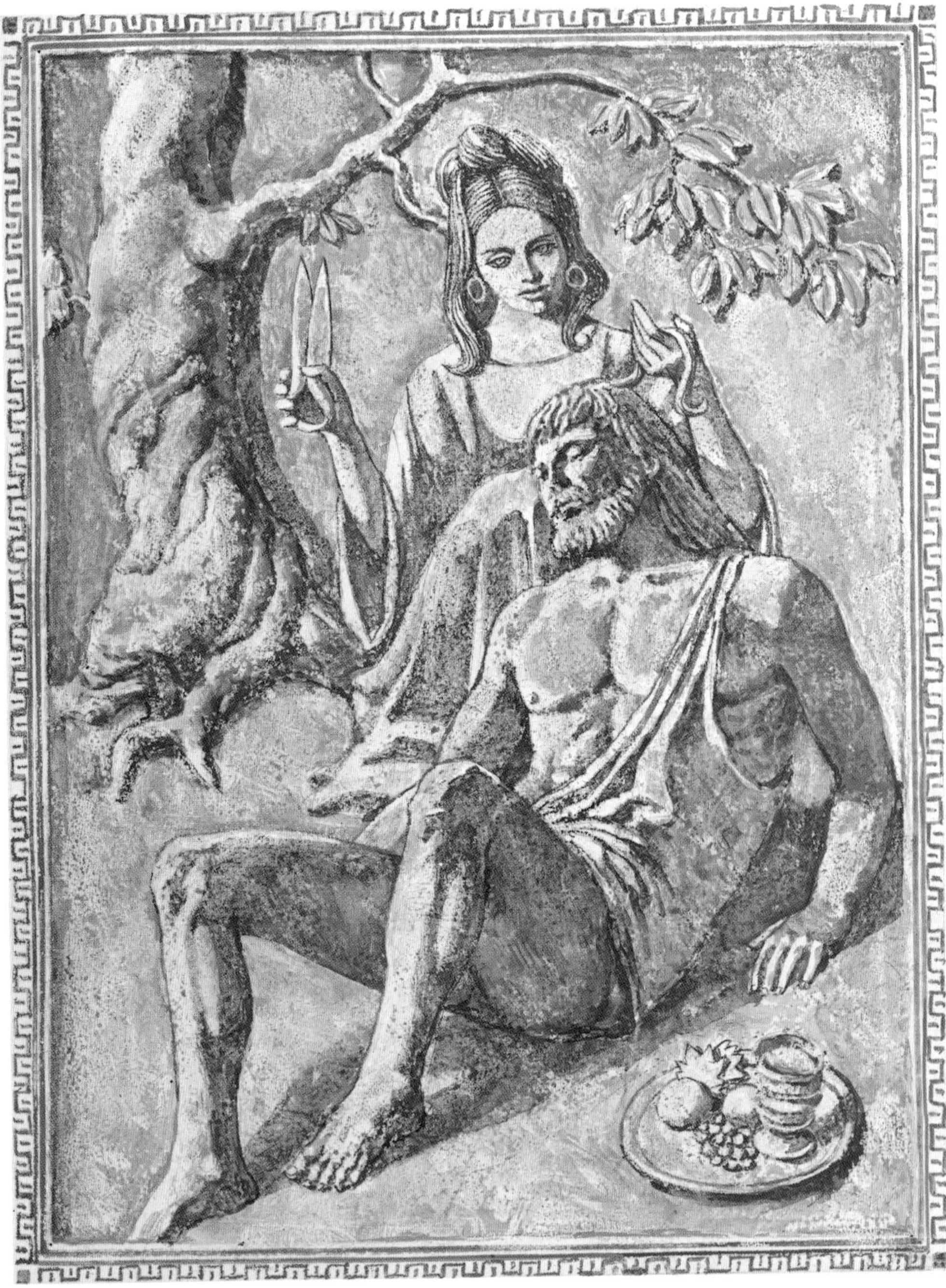

The Serving and the Self-Serving

Take heed, and beware of covetousness: for a man's life consisteth not in the abundance of the things which he possesseth.
— Luke 12:15

The typical woman in the Bible, as in the present day, is a gentle, loving, and charitable creature. The ideal woman is described in Proverbs 31: 20:

"She stretcheth out her hand to the poor; yea, she reacheth forth her hands to the needy." She does not do good for any selfish reason, but because it is a blessing to do good—it blesses the one who receives the benefit, and it blesses the one who confers it:

"Inasmuch as ye have done it unto one of the least of these my brethren," said the Great Teacher, "ye have done it unto me" (Matthew 25:40).

Except for women like Athaliah and Delilah, who were worshipers of false gods, we do not find many selfish women in the Scriptures. Rather, we see a multitude, from Jephthah's poor daughter to the Widow of the Two Mites, who live by the verse "Trust in the Lord and do good" (Psalms 37:3).

Delilah JUDGES 16:4-21

Many men are unfortunate in their choice of the women they love. Few have paid more for their mistakes than Samson did. His last love was the unluckiest of all. For Delilah, the seductress, sold him for money just as Judas did Jesus.

Delilah did not love Samson. She behaved like a harlot and she probably was one. A giant of a man, Samson was doubtless very attractive to Delilah, as he had been to the other women in his life. But the Philistine beauty loved money more.

When the lords of the Philistines heard that Samson, their archenemy, had become a regular visitor at Delilah's house in the valley of Sorek, a delegation of them called on her in secret.

"Entice him," the Philistines said, "and see wherein his great strength lieth, and by what means we may prevail against him, that we may bind him to afflict him: and we will give thee every one of us eleven hundred pieces of silver."

For Delilah, that was a fortune. She went to work on her lover almost at once. "Tell me, I pray thee," she asked him, "wherein thy great strength lieth, and wherewith thou mightest be bound."

Perhaps the hero was so drunk with love that he did not recall how another woman had tried to pry a secret out of him — his wife, the woman of Timnath — with consequences that were terrible for both of them. But more likely he did remember, for he gave Delilah a false answer — he told her he could be bound with green withs (slender, flexible branches). Not long afterward, when Samson was asleep, she tied him with them. She could almost feel the pieces of silver in her hands, but when she woke, all he did was flex his muscles and the withs broke like thread.

Again and again Delilah asked Samson the secret of his strength, and again and again he deceived her — and found, when he awoke, that she had tried to take him prisoner. Perhaps he thought it was all a game. Perhaps he enjoyed matching wits with the enchantress, feeling secure in the possession of his secret.

"How canst thou say, I love thee," Delilah asked the hero, "when thine heart is not with me? thou hast mocked me these three times and hast not told me wherein thy great strength lieth."

Some men cannot hold out against a woman's wheedling, and Samson was one of them. Now, before he knew it, he was saying, "There hath not come a razor upon my head; for I have been a Nazarite unto God from my mother's womb: if I be shaven, then my strength will go from me, and I shall become weak, and be like any other man."

Delilah could see he was telling the truth. As soon as possible, she sent word to the Philistine lords. When they came, they brought eleven hundred pieces of silver.

The siren had just one more scene to play. She lulled her lover to sleep on her knees. As he lay there, she softly called to a man, who came in and shaved Samson's locks off.

Delilah shook the hero. "The Philistines be upon thee, Samson!"

He jumped from the bed. "I will go out as at other times before, and shake myself."

But the Philistines, who were lying in wait, pounced upon him. The Lord had departed from Samson and he was unable to throw them off. He struggled helplessly as his captors held him and put out his eyes.

Delilah was too busy thinking of her money to care.

Samson's Mother JUDGES 13:1-24; 14:2-5, 9, 19

Samson's mother is typical of the good, loyal women whose lives are devoted to their husbands, their children, and God.

The wife of Manoah, a Danite, this gentle woman had been childless for a long time. Then, suddenly, an angel of the Lord appeared to her. "Thou shalt conceive and bear a son," he said. And he proceeded to place special restrictions upon her. She was to avoid strong drink and unclean foods. A razor was never to touch her son's head. He was to be a Nazarite, a man dedicated to God. He was to help deliver Israel out of the hands of the Philistines, who kept them in bondage.

Later the angel appeared again and repeated his instructions, this time to Manoah as well as his wife. In gratitude the pair offered up a burnt sacrifice to the Lord, and the angel ascended to heaven in the flame of the altar.

37

As the angel had predicted, Manoah's wife bore a son. She named him Samson, and he was blessed by the Lord.

When Samson had grown to manhood he told his father and mother he had seen a Philistine woman in Timnath whom he wanted for a wife. He asked them to get her for him, as was the custom.

"Is there never a woman among the daughters of thy brethren, or among all thy people," Manoah complained (and we can be sure his wife joined him), "that thou goest to take a wife of the uncircumcised Philistines?"

But Samson insisted on having his way. Finally his mother and father gave in and went to Timnath. No doubt his mother was at the wedding feast. And no doubt she foresaw that no good would come of the marriage.

She wasn't wrong. Hardly a week had passed before Samson was back in his parents' house. His mother must have welcomed him with cries of joy and perhaps a few I-told-you-so's. But she was not to remain happy for long. She had borne a son who had a great destiny to fulfill, and a grim one.

Athaliah II KINGS 8:26; 11:1-16

Jezebel had a daughter, Athaliah. If ever anyone came close to equaling Jezebel in cruelty and wickedness, it was her own daughter. Like her mother, Athaliah was an idolator and a worshiper of Baal.

For a while, Ahaziah, son of Athaliah, ruled in the kingdom of Judah. Then, like the rest of Ahab's house, he died at the hands of Jehu. When Athaliah heard he was gone, she did not weep for him, as any normal mother would have. One thought, and one thought only, burned in her mind: No one but her little grandsons stood between her and the throne.

Athaliah ordered every one of her grandsons to be put to death. However, one, Joash, was hidden by his aunt, and he escaped the assassins.

Where could the helpless child be kept safe from his terrible grandmother? There was just one place the idolatrous queen could be counted upon not to visit: the temple of Jehovah. The little boy's friends hid him there, under the protection of the high priest, Jehoiada. For years the kingdom suffered under the iron fist of Athaliah and under her false gods. Joash and his protectors waited patiently. When the boy was seven, Jehoiada summoned the princes and the captains of the army to the house of the Lord. He gave them weapons—the shields and swords of King David, which were in the temple. Then he led forth little Joash.

"God save the king!" the assembly cried, and they clapped their hands joyfully.

Hearing the great commotion, the queen hastened to the temple. When she saw the little boy with the crown on his head, surrounded by the cheering crowd, she realized at once what was happening.

"Treason! treason!" she cried.

The captains' hands flew to their sword hilts: Athaliah, dead, would be one threat less to the safety of their boy king. But the high priest stopped them. "Let her not be slain in the house of the Lord," Jehoiada warned. So they led her to the royal palace. And there, at the scene of so many of her own acts of violence, the reign of Queen Athaliah came to an end.

Athaliah's death was a signal for the people to take revenge on her god, Baal. They rushed into the temple, smashed the idols, and killed Baal's priest. Then they tore the temple down, stone by stone.

The cruel queen and her false gods were gone at last. There were few to mourn them.

The Witch of Endor I SAMUEL 28:7-25

The Witch of Endor treated a stricken king with kindness — at the risk of her own life — and so merits a place as an unselfish woman.

The laws of the Jews prohibited sorcery and magic, and King Saul had enforced them. But when he saw an overwhelming host of Philistines gathering to attack his forces and the Lord refused to answer his prayers, a deadly fear took hold of him. He asked his servants to take him to a witch. Since God refused to tell him what his fate would be, perhaps she would.

It was night and Saul was wearing a disguise as he entered the witch's house. She trembled when he told her what he wanted.

"Thou knowest what Saul hath done," the woman answered, "how he hath cut off those that have familiar spirits, and the wizards, out of the land: wherefore then layest thou a snare for my life, to cause me to die?"

"As the Lord liveth, there shall no punishment happen to thee for this thing," Saul replied.

"Whom shall I bring up unto thee?"

"Bring me up Samuel."

When the woman saw Samuel she was struck with awe. She now realized that her visitor was Saul, who had been anointed by the prophet Samuel as Israel's first king. She described the figure of the old man, covered with a mantle and Saul recognized him as Samuel.

"Why hast thou disquieted me?" said the apparition. When the king asked him to draw aside the veil of the future, he heard more than he wanted to. "Tomorrow shalt thou and thy sons be with me: the Lord also shall deliver the host of Israel into the hand of the Philistines."

The king collapsed on the floor. The old woman hobbled over to him. "I have put my life in thy hand," she reminded him. And she begged him to eat — "that thou mayest have strength, when thou goest thy way." With his servants helping, she lifted him onto her bed.

The woman killed a calf — perhaps the only one she had — and baked unleavened bread. Then she fed the king and his servants and they went their way.

We remember the woman of Endor for her seemingly magical powers, but also for the compassion she showed for the once-great king, tottering on the threshold of doom.

40

Ruth and Orpah THE BOOK OF RUTH

The story of Ruth is one of the best loved in the Old Testament. It is also one of the most human, romantic stories in world literature. Like the Book of Esther, it is one of the two books of the Bible (exluding the Apocrypha) that bear the name of a woman.

Ruth was not a daughter of Israel but a native of Moab. Ten years before her story opens, Elimelech and his wife, Naomi, had come from Bethlehem, which was suffering a famine. With them they brought their two sons. The family settled in Moab, a fertile tableland that lies east of the Dead Sea. There their son Mahlon took Ruth as his wife, and his brother, Chilion, married Orpah, another Moabitess.

For a while Elimelech and his family lived contentedly together. Then both he and his two sons died. For Naomi, widowed and childless and old, Moab had lost all of its attractions; she decided to go back to the land of her birth.

"Go, return each to her mother's house," Naomi told her daughters-in-law. "The Lord deal kindly with you, as ye have dealt with the dead, and with me."

Ruth and Orpah wept with the good old woman. She had been like a mother to them. "Surely we will return with thee unto thy people," they told her.

But Naomi urged them to go back to their families. Finally one of them, Orpah, kissed her fondly and left.

Ruth could not be persuaded to do as her sister-in-law had done.

"Intreat me not to leave thee," she told Naomi, "or to return from following after thee: for whither thou goest, I will go; and where thou lodgest, I will lodge: thy people shall be my people, and thy God my God."

So the pair began the long journey to Bethlehem. It was a great distance, and very likely Naomi could not have traveled it without Ruth's help.

The two women settled in Bethlehem. To gain a livelihood for herself and Naomi, Ruth went into the fields at harvest time and followed the reapers, picking the grain they left behind.

One of the fields where Ruth gleaned barley and wheat belonged to a man of wealth, Boaz, who was a kinsman of Elimelech. The pretty young widow did not escape Boaz's eye. His servants told him how she had left her homeland to accompany her aged mother-in-law and now worked to support her.

"Let her glean even among the sheaves, and reproach her not," he advised his young men. "And let also fall some of the handfuls of purpose for her, and leave them, that she may glean them." He also offered her food when he ate in the field.

Naomi was quick to notice that Ruth had brought back much more grain than usual. She learned that her kinsman, Boaz, had shown favor to the young woman. Naomi was determined to provide for Ruth's future and now, at last, she saw a way to do so.

One night Naomi heard that Boaz would be at the threshing floor, winnowing grain. She told Ruth to wash and anoint herself and put on her finest clothes. Then she was to go to the threshing floor and wait until Boaz had finished eating and drinking.

"And it shall be," Naomi told her, "when he lieth down, that thou shalt mark the place where he shall lie, and thou shalt go in, and uncover his feet, and lay thee down; and he will tell thee what thou shalt do."

Ruth followed Naomi's instructions. In the middle of the night Boaz awoke with a start. A strange woman was lying at his feet!

"I am Ruth, thine handmaid," she said calmingly. "Spread therefore thy skirt over thine handmaid; for thou art a near kinsman."

Ruth was following an ancient Jewish custom by which a widow asked a close male relative to take her as his wife. Boaz understood and was flattered. She was an attractive young woman, and she had preferred him to the many young men working in the fields. He told her he would do all that was required of him, and to lie quietly at his feet.

Early in the morning, Ruth left. In her veil she carried six measures of barley, a gift from Boaz to Naomi.

That very day Boaz fulfilled the requirements of the law, and soon Ruth was his happy bride. She was happier still when she bore him a son, whom they named Obed. Naomi's neighbors

42

gathered around her and said of the baby in her arms, "He shall be unto thee a restorer of thy life, and a nourisher of thine old age: for thy daughter in law, which loveth thee, which is better to thee than seven sons, hath born him."

That same baby, grown to manhood, became the father of Jesse, who became the father of David. And from the line of David came Joseph, the husband of Mary, "of whom was born Jesus, who is called Christ" (Matthew 1:16).

So Ruth has come down to us through the ages as the symbol of love and devotion.

The Daughters of Zelophehad NUMBERS 26:33; 27:1-11; 36:1-13; JOSHUA 17:3-6; I CHRONICLES 7:15

Some people acting in their own interests may also benefit others. Although self-serving, they can establish a precedent that may help people for generations to come.

Zelophehad was a wealthy man of the time of Moses. When he died he left five daughters: Mahlah, Noah, Hoglah, Milcah, and Tirzah. He had no sons.

In those days the right of women to inherit was not recognized; only a male could claim an inheritance. To the five daughters it seemed unjust that their father's possessions should pass to his kinsmen, and nothing to them. They took their complaint to Moses at the tabernacle.

"Why should the name of our father be done away from among his family, because he hath no son?" they asked the great leader. "Give unto us therefore a possession among the brethren of our father."

43

Moses stroked his beard. The girls' request seemed reasonable, but the custom was one that had come down through the ages. Whenever he was perplexed, he turned directly to God.

"The daughters of Zelophehad speak right," the Lord told Moses. "Thou shalt surely give them a possession of an inheritance among their father's brethren; and thou shalt cause the inheritance of their father to pass unto them."

Thus it was that, because of the courageous forwardness of the daughters of Zelophehad, daughters came to be treated as equal heirs with sons. Later Moses decreed that the five young women or any other daughters with an inheritance should marry within their father's tribe so his possessions would not pass from his people. Obedient to the prophet's wish, the daughters of Zelophehad married the sons of their father's brothers.

Jephthah's Daughter JUDGES 11:1-40; I SAMUEL 12:11; HEBREWS 11:32

"Jephthah's daughter"—that is all the name she has in the Bible. But her act of self-sacrifice was so unquestioning, so complete, that through the ages it has stood as a symbol of a daughter's devotion to her father.

Jephthah was a man dogged by misfortune from the start. He was the son of Gilead, a man of property. Jephthah's mother was a harlot and his father's other sons felt he had no right to share with them in their inheritance, so they drove Jephthah out. The young man fled to the land of Tob. There he gathered a band of vagabonds about himself and went out on raids with them. He came to be known as an outstanding fighting man among the Jews.

Later the Ammonites, a people of Jordan, made war against Israel. The Israelites needed a general to lead them in their struggle and they thought of Jephthah. The elders of Gilead went to offer him the command.

Perhaps some of Jephthah's half-brothers were among the delegates. For the outcast, it was a moment of triumph." Did ye not hate me and expel me out of my father's house?" he reminded them. "And why are ye come unto me now when ye are in distress?"

In the end Jephthah agreed to march at the head of the Hebrew army. The campaign looked like a dangerous one, and he was not confident he would be victorious. So he swore an oath to the Lord. "If thou shalt without fail deliver the children of Ammon into my hand, then it shall be that whatsoever cometh forth of the doors of my house to meet me, when I return in peace from the children of Ammon, shall surely be the Lord's, and I will offer it up for a burnt offering."

Having made this solemn pledge, Jephthah rode out against the Ammonites. He believed the Lord heard his plea, for one city after another fell to him. The enemy was completely routed.

Lighthearted, Jephthah headed for home. Word of his victory had gone before him. As he rode up to his dwelling a beautiful young woman come forth to meet him, with timbrels and dancing. It was his daughter, his only child.

Jephthah tore his clothes. "Alas, my daughter!" he cried. "Thou hast brought me very low, and thou art one of them that trouble me: for I have opened my mouth unto the Lord, and I cannot go back."

Her feeling of horror, after Jephthah explained, must have been as painful as his. The answer she gave seems almost unbelievable to us, but we must remember we are separated from Jephthah's daughter by thousands of years. In her time a fathers' word was law—especially his word to God.

"My father," she told him, "if thou hast opened thy mouth unto the Lord, do to me according to that which hath proceeded out of thy mouth." She asked only to be allowed to go up into the mountains with her companions to mourn for two months.

At the end of that time Jephthah's daughter returned and her father sorrowfully fulfilled his pledge.

Jephthah's daughter was the only person in the Bible who was sacrificed to Jehovah as a burnt offering. Abraham had been instructed by the Lord to sacrifice Isaac, as a test of his faith but the Lord substituted a ram for the sacrifice.

45

The Power of Courage

I gave my back to the smiters, and my cheeks to them that plucked off the hair: I hid not my face from shame and spitting. For the Lord God will help me; therefore shall I not be confounded: therefore have I set my face like a flint, and I know that I shall not be ashamed.

—— Isaiah 50:6-7

In dark moments, one may gain strength and support by thinking of the women of the Bible and of the dangers and tragedies that surrounded them on every hand. Esther saved her people from annihilation. Rahab the harlot was instrumental in making Joshua's attack on Jericho successful. Deborah was so revered that the chieftain of the Hebrews would not go to battle unless she would consent to accompany his fighting men. These women and others, lived in a far crueler world than we do, and they faced its terrors with a quality of courage that can still inspire us today.

Not every woman in the Bible was a heroine. Some, like Job's wife, gave up as one disaster after another was heaped upon them. They had forgotten a great but simple truth — that courage is ours for the asking.

"Whoso putteth his trust in the Lord shall be safe." (Proverbs 29:25).

Deborah and Jael JUDGES 4:4-24

Unlike other people of Old Testament times, the children of Israel treated their women with deep respect. In their society a woman was eligible to hold almost any position. Nor did she have to give up any of her womanliness. She could even be a prophetess and a mother at the same time. One of the heroic prophetesses of the Bible was a mother of Israel named Deborah.

The children of Israel had been oppressed by the king of Canaan for twenty years when the Lord revealed to Deborah that the time had come to strike a blow for liberty. So she sent for Barak, a chieftain of the Hebrews, and urged him to do battle with Sisera, the Canaanite general.

The Bible gives us few testimonials to the power of a woman as impressive as the answer Barak made to Deborah. "If thou wilt go with me, then I will go: but if thou wilt not go with me, then I will not go." Radiating courage and faith in the Lord, the prophetess had the ability to lift up the hearts of all those around her.

Deborah went forth with Barak's army and they attacked Sisera and his chariots. His mighty host vanquished, Sisera himself was compelled to flee on foot.

Just as one woman had inspired the Israelites to rise up against Sisera, another was to destroy him with her own hand. This was Jael, the wife of Heber.

Sisera came to Jael's tent and asked her for refuge. "Turn in, my lord, turn into me; fear not," she told him. And she hid him in her tent.

But Jael knew that Sisera was an enemy of the Lord's people and they would never have peace as long as he lived. So, while the enemy general slept, she took a nail and drove it through his head.

Thanks to the courage and patriotism of these two women, the children of Israel were free at last, and the land had peace for many years.

Pilate's Wife MATTHEW 27:19

We meet her in just a single verse in the New Testament—but the words she spoke in that verse not only made her immortal but helped to make her a saint in the Greek Orthodox Church. Like Lot's wife, she is known only by her husband's name, although tradition says she was called Claudia Procula.

Pilate, Roman governor of Judaea, was preparing to judge Jesus when a servant came from his wife with this message: "Have thou nothing to do with that just man: for I have suffered many things this day in a dream because of him."

Some say she was a secret Christian and that was why she spoke out so emphatically to her husband. Her courgeous words carried so much weight with Pilate that he pleaded with the multitude to spare the life of the Saviour.

Esther and Vashti THE BOOK OF ESTHER

Esther was one of the bravest women in the Bible. She was gifted with beauty and grace, but her courage surpassed them both. Because she used her courage with the wisdom of a woman — with prudence and modesty — she was able to achieve something no other woman has ever done. She saved a whole people from destruction.

It happened during the Babylonian exile. Ahasuerus, king of the Persians, who held the children of Israel captive, was a vain, cruel man. Once he gave a feast in his palace at Shushan. After his guests had admired his wealth and his possessions, the drunken king decided he would prade before them his greatest prize — his lovely queen, Vashti. But Vashti refused: she felt she could not obey the king's request and preserve her dignity as a woman. For that refusal Ahasuerus sent her away.

The king needed a new queen, and virgins were brought from everywhere in his vast empire to compete for his favor. One of these was Esther, the adopted daughter of a pious Israelite named Mordecai. Her name in Hebrew, Hadassah, means myrtle. When Mordecai sent Esther to the royal harem, he cautioned her to keep secret the name of her people and her kindred.

Of all the maidens who came to the king's palace, Esther pleased Ahasuerus most. He made her his queen and never knew she was a daughter of Israel.

49

Mordecai spent much of his time at the palace gate, trying to pick up news of Esther. One day he overheard a plot to kill Ahasuerus. He sent word to Esther, who warned the king in time, and Mordecai's name was written in the royal chronicles, although he was never rewarded.

Ahasuerus had a favorite, Haman, whom he placed above all the princes of the empire. To do Haman honor, the king commanded that all should bow before him. Mordecai was the only one to refuse.

In Haman's eyes, this refusal was a crime. It angered him so much that he resolved not just Mordecai, but every Jew in the empire, should pay with his life for it. The king readily agreed that the Jews should be put to death and an order was issued to massacre them on a certain date.

Somehow a copy of the order fell into Mordecai's hands. He told Esther she had to plead with Ahasuerus and save her people. "Who knoweth whether thou art come to the kingdom for such a time as this?" he said.

No one was allowed to enter the king's presence unbidden on pain of death. Esther had no choice—she had to risk the king's displeasure or she might not get to him in time. "And if I perish," she told Mordecai, "I perish."

Fortunately, the king received his lovely queen affectionately. Wisely, Esther did not reveal her purpose at once. Instead, she invited Ahasuerus and Haman to a banquet. Haman was deeply flattered, but when he left the palace, there was Mordecai, still refusing to bow. Haman ordered a lofty gallows to be erected: on it, the accursed Hebrew would pay for his insults to the king's favorite.

That night Ahasuerus was unable to sleep. He asked that his chronicles be read to him and from them he learned how Mordecai had saved his life. In recognition of such a service the king gave orders that honors should be lavished upon Mordecai. We can imagine the rage Haman felt when he learned of his enemy's good fortune.

But Haman was to suffer a more severe blow at the banquet the queen gave for him and Ahasuerus. She told the king she was a Hebrew and that Haman had plotted to destroy her and all her people.

"If I have found favour in thy sight, O king, and if it please the king," she said, "let my life be given me at my petition, and my people at my request."

When Haman, fearful of losing the king's favor, begged Esther to take pity on him, he seemed to be assaulting her. The king, in his wrath, ordered Haman to be hanged on the gallows he had built for Mordecai.

For the children of Israel an era of safety and prosperity dawned. Their descendants have never forgotten Queen Esther, and they commemorate the day she saved them with a holiday, the feast of Purim. On that day, in synagogues around the world, they read the Book of Esther aloud—one of the two books in the Bible named for a woman.

Job's Wife JOB 2:9-10

The Bible gives us many pictures of women who stood firm in the face of adversity, but few of women who were faint-hearted. Perhaps the most pathetic of these is Job's wife.

Job was "perfect and upright, and one that feared God and eschewed evil." When Satan told the Lord that it was natural for Job to honor Him since He had bestowed many blessings upon him, the Lord gave Satan permission to try Job's faith. The Devil went to work eagerly. He stripped his innocent victim of his possessions, his children, and his health.

Job did not lose trust in the goodness of God, but his poor wife did. "Dost thou still retain thy integrity?" she asked her husband. "Curse God and die."

"Thou speakest as one of the foolish women speaketh," Job replied. "What? shall we receive good at the hand of God, and shall we not receive evil?"

51

He could not see God's purpose, but, unlike his faint-hearted wife, his faith in the Lord persevered.

Naomi BOOK OF RUTH

Another woman whose courage ran low because she thought the Lord had turned against her was Naomi. Naomi had lost her husband, and then she lost her two sons. Her home was in an alien land, Moab, and her age and poverty weighed heavily upon her.

With her devoted daughter-in-law, Ruth, Naomi returned to her native land. When her old friends saw her, she was so changed that they asked, "Is this Naomi?" "Call me not Naomi . . . ," she replied. Naomi means "pleasant in Hebrew; the suffering woman asked to be called Mara or "bitter" instead—"for the Almighty hath dealt very bitterly with me. I went out full, and the Lord hath brought me home again empty."

Better days were coming. Naomi helped her daughter-in-law find a husband and in time Ruth bore a son. That son, Obed, was a joy and a comfort to Naomi as long as she lived.

Lydia   ACTS 16:14-15, 40

When the apostle Paul brought the Gospel to Europe, the first city he taught in was Philippi, in Macedonia. Here he met Lydia, a merchant who sold purple goods. God opened her heart and she accepted the new religion. Paul baptized her and all her household.

"Come into my house, and abide there," Lydia said to Paul. And ever afterward her home was a meeting place for Christians and a shelter for the faithful.

Lydia's public spirit and courage helped to plant the word of God firmly in the pagan soil of Europe. It was to Lydia and other "saints" like her that Paul wrote his Epistle to the Philippians from prison.

Rahab   JOSHUA 2:1-21; 6:17-25; HEBREWS 11:31; JAMES 2:25

Rahab was a harlot, but so firm was her faith in the Lord and so excellent were her works for His people that she redeemed herself. Even Peter and James spoke of her with reverence.

Rahab's dwelling place was in the wall of the city of Jericho. Before Joshua led his army against the city, he sent spies to study the land. Rahab gave them shelter.

Word got out that there were spies in the city. The kings' soldiers came to Rahab and asked if she had seen them, but she sent the soldiers off on a wild goose chase. For her kindness, the Hebrew spies promised to spare her and her family on the day their army attacked the city. When their work was completed she let them down from her window by a scarlet cord and they stole away to report to Joshua.

On the day the Israelites stormed the city that same cord hung in Rahab's window—a sign to them to spare her and hers. The invaders, forewarned, respected the cord. "By faith," said the apostle Paul, "the harlot Rahab perished not with them that believed not."

The Widow of the Two Mites MARK 12:41-44

One day Jesus sat down opposite the treasure chest of the temple in Jerusalem and watched people dropping contributions into it. Wealthy men came up and emptied large purses into the chest. Then He saw a poor widow stop at the chest. She shook two little coins into the palm of her hand and carefully dropped them in.

This was something for His disciples to know about. He called them to him.

"This poor widow," the Great Teacher said, "hath cast more in, than all they which have cast into the treasury: for all they did cast in of their abundance; but she of her want did cast in all that she had, even all her living."

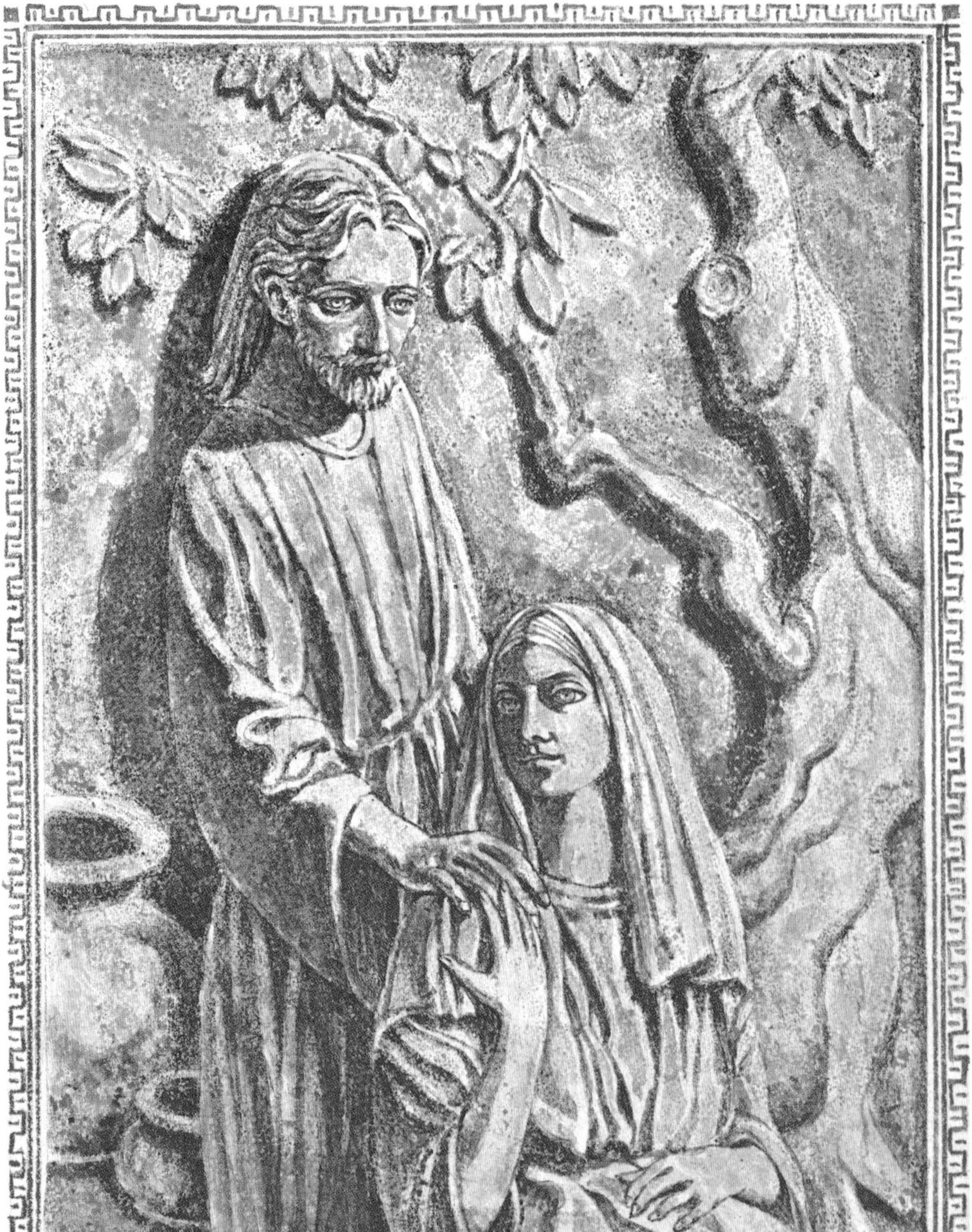

Love and Hate

Hatred stirreth up strifes: but love covereth all sins.

— Proverbs 10:12

Better is a dinner of herbs where love is, than a stalled ox and hatred therewith.

— Proverbs 15:17

In the Scriptures we see many portraits of women who love, but few of women who hate. Sarah could not tolerate Hagar, but she was not a hateful woman by nature; Hagar goaded her to it. Rachel turned against her father, but only because he had not treated her and her husband, Jacob, fairly. Even Jezebel, cruel and shameless as she was, and a worshiper of false gods, seems to have been a dutiful wife to her husband, Ahab.

Most of the women we see in any detail in the Bible love their God. They love their country. They love their fathers and their mothers. They love their husbands. But most of all they love their children.

The Bible is full of incomparable portraits of loving mothers. Mothers play an important role in the Scriptures because they play an important role in life. Our mothers are the first people who love us and the first people we love in return. No matter what we do in life, they keep on loving us.

The greatest woman in either of the Testaments is a loving mother—Mary, mother of Jesus.

Mother is another word for love.

55

Mary, Mother of Jesus MATTHEW 1:16, 18-25; 2:11; 13:55; LUKE 1:26-35; 2:41-49; JOHN 2:1-12; ACTS 1:14

"There is no rose of such virtue," says a very old English song, "as is the rose that bare Jesu."

Next to Jesus, Mary is the most revered figure in the New Testament. Great music, poetry, and art have been inspired by her. Countless churches and cathedrals have been erected in her honor around the world, and great treasures presented to them in her name. Yet Mary herself, the Holy Mother, was the humblest of the humble — a sweet and loving soul chosen for a great mission by the Lord.

According to some tradition, Mary was the daughter of St. Joachim and St. Anne. Her birth was a miraculous one, for her parents were elderly when she came into the world. Some of the mothers in the Old Testament, like Sarah and Hannah, also bore their children with the help of the Lord.

Mary first learned that she was to be the mother of the Son of God when the archangel Gabriel appeared to her. "Hail, thou that art highly favoured," he greeted Mary, "the Lord is with thee: blessed art thou among women." And he went on to tell her the Holy Ghost would come to her and she would conceive and bring forth a son, who would be called Jesus.

After the Annunciation, Mary went to her elderly cousin Elisabeth to share her news with her. Gabriel had already appeared to Elisabeth, revealing that she, too, would bear a son. Seeing Mary, Elisabeth was filled with the Holy Ghost.

"Blessed art thou among women, and blessed is the fruit of thy womb," she greeted her cousin.

"My soul doth magnify the Lord," Mary replied. "And my soul hath rejoiced in God my Saviour".

Her words of praise to God form a superb hymn, known as the *Magnificat*.

Later Mary, already big with child, had to go with her betrothed husband, Joseph, to Bethlehem, to be taxed. The couple was unable to find lodging in the crowded city, so Jesus was born in a stable. Miracles attended the birth: an angel summoned shepherds to pay homage to the Infant and a star led three kings of the East to the stable in Bethlehem. For Mary, these extraordinary events confirmed the message she had received from the lips of the archangel.

Soon afterward Mary came to the temple at Jerusalem with

Joseph to present her firstborn son to the Lord. Anna and Simeon, two holy people, prophesied the child would do great things in Israel. "Yea, a sword shall pierce through thy own soul also," Simeon told the wondering young mother.

Almost at once it seemed as if Simeon's words were about to come true. An insane monarch, Herod, sat on the throne. Hearing that a king had been born to the Jews, he ordered all baby boys to be slain so he would not have to fear any rival. With Joseph and her baby, Mary fled to Egypt. They remained in hiding there until Herod died.

The childhood of Jesus may have been much like any other. He played in His father's carpenter shop in Nazareth and learned to help him. A poet has given us a memorable picture of this time:

Day

Followed on day, like any childhood's passing:
And silently sat Mary at her wheel,
And watched the boy-Messiah as she spun;
And as a human child unto its mother
Subject the while, He did her low voice bidding—
Or gently came to lean upon her knee,
And ask her of the thoughts that in Him stirred
Dimly as yet—or with affection sweet,
Tell, murm'ring of His weariness—and then,
All tearful-hearted (as a human mother
Unutterably fond, while touched with awe),
She paused, or with tremulous hand spun on—

When Jesus was twelve, His parents took Him to the temple in Jerusalem as they did every year, to celebrate the Passover feast. They traveled with a group of relatives, and when they set out for home, they felt sure the Child was with them. After a while, when they went to look for Him, they could not find Him. They hastened back to Jerusalem, searching along the way.

After three days, Joseph and Mary found the Boy in the temple at Jerusalem, sitting with the learned men.

"Son, why hast thou thus dealt with us?" his mother asked. "Behold, thy father and I have sought thee sorrowing."

"How is it that ye sought me?" Jesus answered. "Wist ye not that I must be about my Father's business?" In this way He reminded Mary that He had a special purpose to fulfill on earth.

Mary was present when Jesus, now a grown man, performed the first of His miracles. He and His disciples had been invited to a marriage at Cana, in Galilee. Mary noticed that all the wine jars had been emptied. "They have no wine," she said to Jesus.

"Woman, what have I to do with thee?" Jesus replied. He was telling her again that His responsibility was not to her or to anyone else earthly, but to God on high. "Mine hour is not yet come." Even so, He had heard her words and to the astonishment of the wedding party, He transformed six pots of water into wine.

On another occasion, Jesus was traveling with His disciples and His mother and His brethren came to visit him. A multitude of eager listeners surrounded the Master in the house where He was teaching.

"Behold, thy mother and thy brethren without seek for thee," Jesus was told.

"Who is my mother, or my brethren?" the Master asked. And He told the crowd that everyone present was as close to Him as His mother and His brethren. "For whosoever shall do the will of my father, the same is my brother, and my sister, and mother."

Perhaps his words sound harsh, but Mary, who knew as well as He that he had a mission, must have understood. She had borne Jesus not for herself but for the world.

Mary, in love, followed her son unhesitatingly. She was at the foot of the cross during His last earthly moments. Here Jesus's love for His mother reasserted itself. He knew she would need someone to take care of her after He was gone. His favorite disciple, John, was standing near at hand. "Woman, behold thy son!" Jesus said. And, to John: "Behold thy mother!" Afterward John took Mary into his own home.

Mary cherished the teachings of her Son and Saviour. Our last glimpse of her is in the Upper Room in Jerusalem, where we see her praying with the disciples, after the Ascension. Her soul had been pierced by a sword, as Simeon had prophesied long ago, but she could take comfort in the knowledge that God, through her, had given new hope and happiness to mankind.

The Two Mothers I KINGS 3:16-28

The Bible shows us many remarkable pictures of mother love. One of the most dramatic is the story of the two mothers in the First Book of Kings.

Although everyone reveres motherhood, virtue is not one of its qualifications. Sometimes mothers can be harlots, like the two women in this tale. The Bible makes no mention of the fathers of the children the women bore. Perhaps the harlots themselves did not know who they were.

The two women lived alone in the same house. Both had become pregnant at about the same time. Finally one of the women gave birth to a lusty, lively boy. She was very happy to have him.

Three days later the second woman's time came. The women must have helped each other with the births; there was no one else in the house. The second woman was also delivered of a son.

Next morning the first mother opened her eyes. Her waking thought was of the baby at her side. He seemed strangely quiet. Horrified, she saw the child was not breathing.

Almost at the same instant she realized the dead little boy was not her son. No one knows a baby like its own mother. The child, she could see, was her neighbor's.

Anxiously she hurried to the other woman's room. The second woman was holding a child at her breast. One glance at the infant told the first mother it was her own son. But the second mother hotly denied it.

A furious argument began. The two were still arguing weeks later when they were brought before the highest judge in the land —King Solomon himself.

"This woman's child died in the night," the first mother testified

59

to the king, "because she overlaid it. And she arose at midnight, and took my son from beside me, while thine handmaid slept, and laid it in her bosom, and laid her dead child in my bosom."

"Nay," said the second woman, "but the living is my son, and the dead is thy son."

There were no other witnesses. No evidence but the word of one deeply involved against the word of the other.

The king had a reputation for wisdom. But here was a case that seemed to be beyond even the wisdom of a Solomon. The people in the court whispered among themselves.

"Bring me a sword."

Had the king really spoken those words? What could he want a sword for?

The weapon was fetched. The king cleared his throat. "Divide the living child in two, and give half to the one, and half to the other."

"O my lord—" It was the first mother, sobbing. "Give her the living child, and in no wise slay it."

The second mother coldly disagreed with her. "Let it be neither mine nor thine, but divide it."

The audience gasped. The two women's spontaneous reactions to Solomon's order had revealed the truth. A child's real mother would never ask that it be divided!

The king pointed to the first woman. "Give her the living child, and in no wise slay it: she is the mother thereof."

Two mothers. One who loved the child because it was hers. One who was willing to see it die because it was not.

60

Rachel and Leah

GENESIS 29:6-35; 30:1-6, 22-24;
31:1-3, 17-35; 35:16-18
JEREMIAH 31:15; MATTHEW 2:18

Jacob was given a new name by God: Israel, which means prevailing with God, or God rules. The Jews were called the children of Israel in his honor. They regarded him as the father of their nation—but if he was their father, his two faithful wives Rachel and Leah, have good right to be called their mothers. For those two "did build the house of Israel." (Ruth 4:11).

Rachel and Leah were sisters. Rachel was younger and prettier. Once Jacob had seen her he could not get her out of his mind, and he finally asked for her hand in marriage. "I will serve thee seven years for Rachel, thy younger daughter," he told her father, Laban.

To Jacob the seven years must have seemed almost like seventy. When they were over, Laban made a feast. Jacob waited in the dark for his bride and she came to him. But in the morning he discovered Laban had tricked him: his bride was Leah, not Rachel. Justifying himself, Laban explained that it was the custom of the country that the younger daughter could not be married before the older.

For Jacob it was a stinging disappointment. But Laban told him he could have Rachel in a week if he agreed to work for another seven years. Jacob had no choice but to agree, for Rachel was the woman he loved.

It was one of the ironies of Jacob's life that Leah, for whom he did not care deeply, bore him son after son, but Rachel, his darling, was childless. She loved her husband and her barrenness tormented her. "Give me children," she told Jacob, "or else I die." Following the ancient custom, she had him marry Bilhah, her handmaid. "She shall bear upon my knees," said Rachel, "that I may also have children by her."

Jacob's house began to fill up with sons, but still none was Rachel's. Then, as the Book of Genesis says, "God remembered Rachel." She bore a son, whom she named Joseph. The boy was to grow up to be a great leader of his people.

61

Not long after Joseph was born, God ordered Jacob to return to his homeland. While Laban was away, Jacob fled with his family and servants, taking half of Laban's flocks. Rachel must have smiled as they left. Hidden among her possessions were her father's household images. These statues, in Jacob's hands, would guarantee his title to the livestock he had taken from Laban.

Three days later, Laban was on the fugitives' trail. In a week, on Mount Gilead, he and his followers overtook them. He was furious. He raged against Jacob for stealing his daughters and his grandchildren and his flocks. He was especially angry because his household images, too, had been carried off.

Rachel had never told her husband she had her father's images. So it is not surprising that Jacob readily gave Laban permission to search his possessions—and to kill whoever he found had the goods. When Laban strode into Rachel's tent she didn't get up. He turned everything topsy-turvy. Still he could not find them and finally he went away. He never suspected that his daughter had been sitting on them all the time!

Rachel was to bear her husband another son, Benjamin. She died in childbirth—the first woman mentioned in the Bible to do so.

Jacob had twelve sons in all from Rachel, Leah and his concubines, each of whom founded one of the twelve tribes of Israel.

Herodias and Salome MATTHEW 14:3-12; MARK 6:17-28

Herodias will always be remembered not as a woman who loved but as one who hated. Curiously enough, the object of her hatred was a saint.

Herod Antipas was the tetrarch of Galilee when Jesus was put to death. He coveted Herodias, who was his brother's wife. Finally Herodias divorced her husband, Herod Antipas put away his wife, and the two lovers were married. Their conduct made many enemies for them.

One of those who cried out against the pair was John the Baptist. "It is not lawful for thee to have thy brother's wife!" John reminded Herod again and again.

John's angry words had little effect on Herod, but they stirred up the wrath of his wife. Herodias demanded that John the Baptist should be executed. Herod was unwilling to take the holy man's life, for he had many followers, but he locked him up in prison.

Herodias could be satisfied with nothing less than John's death. She waited impatiently for her opportunity.

It came, at last, on the tetrarch's birthday. Herodias's daughter by her first marriage, Salome, had danced for Herod and pleased him greatly. "Ask of me whatsoever thou wilt, and I will give it thee," he told his stepdaughter.

Salome could not think of what to ask, so she consulted her mother.

"The head of John the Baptist," replied Herodias instantly.

Herod did not want to kill the prophet, but he had given Salome his solemn promise that she could have anything she asked. John's head was delivered to her on a platter.

As soon as Salome received the head, she carried it to her mother.

To anyone else the gift would have been a grisly one. To Herodias, however, it was a symbol of her final triumph over the man she hated.

Rizpah II II SAMUEL 3:7; 21:8-14

Women show their love in different ways, at different times. Rizpah won a place in the Bible story by the extraordinary way she showed hers. Rizpah, a concubine of King Saul, bore him two sons. After Saul's death the Gibeonites wanted to take revenge on Saul's family for the wrongs he had done them. They asked King David for Rizpah's two sons and the five sons of Saul's daughter Merab. David turned over the seven men to the Gibeonites who hanged them.

It was an excruciating painful sight for the mother to see her sons' dead bodies swinging in the wind. Taking some sackcloth, Rizpah spread it on a rock nearby and sat there. When animals or birds came close to the hanging bodies she drove them off. Day after day she remained on her rock in the wind and the rain. Watching. Guarding.

At long last, word of Rizpah's devotion to the dead sons was brought to King David. He ordered that their bones be taken

63

down and given an honorable burial with those of Saul and Jonathan.

Rizpah had not stood guard in vain over the ones she had loved and lost.

The Woman of Timnath JUDGES 14; 15:1-8

Love calls for openness and a willingness to give of oneself. It calls for understanding and complete trust. If there is any holding back, it can destroy a marriage.

Samson was a man of great strength, the Hercules of the Jews. One day he saw a young Philistine woman of Timnath and fell in love with her. Like fathers and mothers in every age, his parents warned him not to take a woman of another people. That only made him angry. "Get her for me; for she pleaseth me well," he told Manoah, his father.

On his way to Timnath, the hero was attacked by a young lion. The Lord lent him strength; with his bare hands he wrung the beast's neck. Later, when he passed by the same place, he was surpised to find a swarm of bees and honey in the carcass. He ate some of the honey and he gave some to his mother and father.

Many young Philistines came to Samson's wedding feast. At the start of the seven-day celebration the groom proposed a riddle to them. "Out of the eater came forth meat and out of the strong came forth sweetness." If the Philistines could guess the answer by the end of the seven days, Samson told them, he would give them thirty sheets and thirty changes of garments. If not, they had to give the same prize to him.

It was a difficult riddle—too difficult for the Philistines—but they didn't intend to lose. They cornered Samson's wife. If she did not find out the answer from Samson and tell them, they swore they would burn down the house, with her inside.

A loving, trusting wife would have rushed to her husband and told him everything, but the woman of Timnath hardly knew Samson, and she was afraid of her countrymen. So she went to him and wept and wheedled. "Thou dost but hate me, and lovest me not: thou hast put forth a riddle unto the children of my people, and hast not told it me."

Day after day she carried on. Finally Samson could stand it no longer. As soon as he gave her the answer she ran off to report it to her countrymen.

When the Philistines told Samson the solution to his riddle, he understood at once how they had learned it. "If ye had not plowed with my heifer, ye had not found out my riddle," he said. After giving them the promised prize he deserted his bride.

It was not long before Samson regretted his haste and he came back, only to find the woman of Timnath was gone. She had been married to another man. His rage demanded an outlet—and he found it in setting fire to the Philistines' crops.

"Who hath done this?" screamed the Philistines. They soon found out and because Samson's anger had been unleashed by the woman of Timnath and her father, they burned both of them to death.

So one wrong led to another and another. Before the feud between Samson and the Philistines came to an end, many had died. All because his wife had not loved or trusted him enough to tell him the truth.

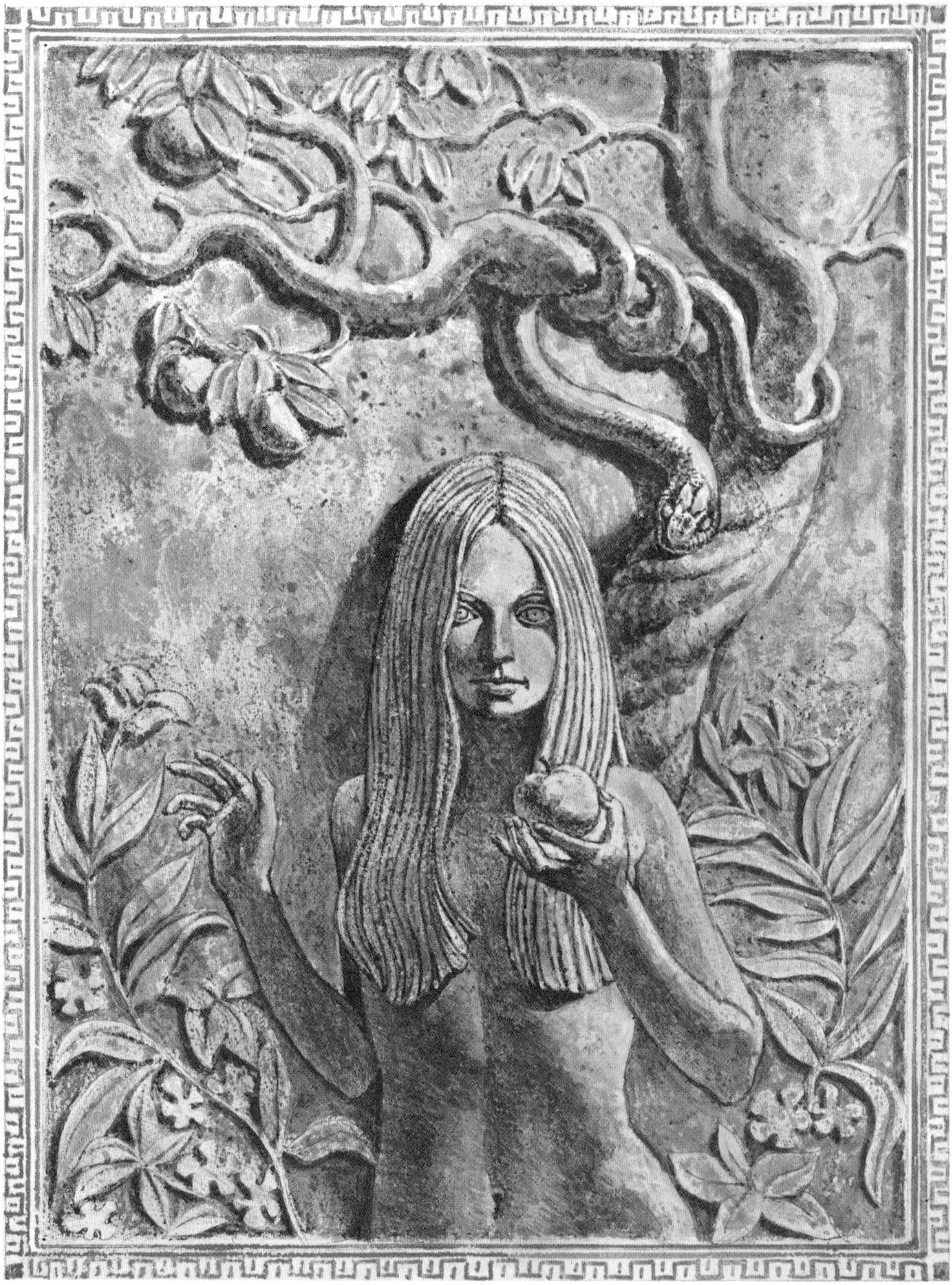

Women of Wisdom, Women of Folly

The wise shall inherit glory.

Proverbs 3:35

Ye suffer fools gladly, seeing ye yourselves are wise.

II Corinthians 11:19

The women of the Bible provide us with many examples of gentle wisdom. Jochebed, mother of Moses is remembered for the resourcefulness with which she protected her child. From Mary, mother of Jesus, we learn to bear our trials with faith. Abigail teaches us the virtues of tact and diplomacy. The Queen of Sheba exhibits one of the characteristics of a truly wise person: She is willing to listen and learn from another—and is content with only first-hand knowledge rather than hearsay.

We can learn almost as much from the foolish women of the Bible, for their misfortunes make us aware of the pitfalls of life. Eve's vain wish to be as knowledgeable as a god, merely made her more human and vulnerable. Lot's wife also paid severely for her disobedience. Rebekah believed she could deceive her husband, Isaac. These women suffered from their mistakes—and give others a chance to learn from them.

Eve GENESIS 2:17-25; 3:1-13, 16-24

Her name, in Hebrew, means life. It is a good name for the first woman, the mother of us all. Artists through the ages have pictured her as a woman of surpassing loveliness.

Yet if Eve was a great beauty, she was also a great and foolish sinner. She was the first person to disobey a command of the Lord. Because of her folly, and her husband's, the race of man was expelled from paradise.

Eve did not disobey the Lord because she was a depraved or

67

wicked person. Her sin was rooted in weakness of will—she was too gullible, too easily persuaded. Even in the Garden of Eden there was a bad companion, eager to lead her astray. We can almost see the first woman, as in some old woodcut, bending her graceful head, her innocent eyes open wide as she listens to the evil one.

"Now the serpent," says the Bible, "was more subtil than any beast of the field, which the Lord God had made." Eve, intent on the serpent's words, could not have seen the malevolent glitter in his eye as he assured her no harm would befall her if she ate of the fruit of the tree of knowedge. Rather, it woud make her wise as a god.

Eve did not know the serpent, but the serpent knew Eve. And so he played upon a basic weakness of hers. Human beings always want to be more than they are. We would like to be as gods, superbly powerful, all-knowing, immortal. Who of us could resist tasting the forbidden fruit if he believed it would make him divine?

Not only did Eve taste the fruit—she gave some to Adam. No doubt the serpent, watched with approval: she was doing his work of wickedness for him.

The fruit was delicious, but suddenly they found it had taken their original innocence from them. They covered their nakedness and hid themselves from the Lord.

God found them and asked Adam: "Hast thou eaten of the tree, whereof I commanded thee that thou shouldest not eat?"

The man hung his head and blamed the woman. The woman was equally quick to pass the blame. "The serpent beguiled me, and I did eat."

God condemned them to a life of hardship. "In the sweat of thy face shalt thou eat bread, till thou return unto the ground." They were shut out of the Garden of Eden forever.

Eve, our first mother, is a tragic figure. Her tragedy was the result of her weakness of will and her desire for greatness—and also of her influence over the man. All the serpent had to do was win Eve over, and Adam was sure to fall.

In spite of her folly, and the anguish with which she paid for it, Eve was a great woman. She was the helper and the mate of the first man. She was the mother of mankind. Like Adam, she was made in the image of God, by His own hand. She was touched by the divinity of that hand and so is every last one of her daughters.

Abigail I SAMUEL 25:1-42

Of all the great women in the Old Testament, few can equal Abigail in wisdom. She was a peacemaker. Abigail knew how angry and childish men could be—and she knew how to handle them with insight and diplomacy so they would come to themselves quickly.

But not her husband, Nabal. Even the wisest woman could do nothing with him.

A wealthy owner of great flocks, Nabal was greedy and thoughtless. When the young David and his men were hiding in the wilderness from King Saul, they often helped Nabal's shepherds to protect their flocks. Later, at shearing time—a time of feasting—David sent some of his young men to ask for provisions. It would have been no more than fair to grant his request. But the miserly Nabal thought otherwise. "Who is David?" he grunted viciously, and he sent David's men away with empty hands.

David was furious when he heard. "Gird ye on every man his sword!" he roared, and he reached for his own. Only blood could wash away such an insult.

69

But one of the young men told Abigail how unjustly her husband had treated David's request. Without a word to Nabal, she ordered her servants to load ample provisions on asses. Then she headed for David's camp.

When Abigail found the young warrior, she bowed to the ground before him. David's fury turned to wonder as he heard Abigail apologize for her husband's folly and he saw the food and wine she had brought for him and his men.

He was deeply grateful. "Blessed be thou, which hast kept me this day from coming to shed blood," David said, "and from avenging myself with mine own hand."

So, because of his wife's tact and understanding, Nabal escaped David's anger, but he could not escape the Lord's. When Abigail returned home and told her husband what she had done, he was struck dumb "and he became as a stone." Ten days later he was dead.

Abigail did not remain a widow for long. Hearing of Nabal's fate, David gave thanks to God for taking the young warrior's revenge into His own hand. And he sent messengers to Abigail to tell her he wanted her to be his wife.

Rebekah GENESIS 27:1-43

Many a mother has made the mistake of favoring one child over the other. If one child is gentle and loving and the other rough and independent, the snare is already set for her.

Rebekah favored her gentle second-born son, Jacob. Her husband, Isaac, favored the first-born, Esau, a rugged man of the outdoors.

One day Rebekah heard Isaac, who was old and blind, ask Esau to kill a deer and make a dish of venison for him. "Bring it to me, that I may eat; that my soul may bless thee before I die," Isaac said.

With a father's blessing went a greater share of his possessions and special honor. Rebekah wanted that blessing for her younger boy. So, while Esau was out hunting for the deer, she told Jacob to kill two young goats. And she made a savory dish of the meat, such as her husband loved. Then she dressed Jacob in Esau's clothes, with their outdoor smell. And, because Esau was hairy, she placed the skin of the goats on Jacob's hands and neck, so he would feel like Esau to his blind father's touch.

Jacob carried the steaming dish of meat to his father. Old Isaac could not see, but he could hear, and the voice he heard was not his older son's. He touched Jacob. "The voice is Jacob's voice," the old man muttered uneasily, "but the hands are the hands of Esau." Then he smelled the smell of the fields on Esau's clothes, which Jacob was wearing, and his doubts vanished. And so he gave Jacob the blessing that rightfully belonged to Esau.

Jacob's act of deceit brought his brother's wrath down upon him. Esau swore Jacob would pay for his treachery with his life. To protect her favorite, Rebekah had to send him away to his uncle's house, where he sojourned for many years.

For Rebekah, those must have been years of sharp regret. Her beloved second-born was far away, she could not see him or hear his voice. Old Isaac had doubtless discovered how she had helped Jacob trick the blessing out of him, and he could not have loved her better for it. And whenever she saw Esau and remembered what she had done, day must have turned to night for her.

Lot's Wife GENESIS 19:15-26

She is one of the most widely known of Old Testament women, yet no one knows her name. Even Jesus called her by her husband's name when He admonished His disciples, "Remember Lot's wife" (Luke 17:32).

Lot was the nephew of the patriarch Abraham, and he dwelt in Sodom, one of the wicked cities of the plain. When the Lord, appalled by the depravity of those cities, resolved to destroy them, He sent His angels to warn Lot and his family. "Escape for thy life; look not behind thee," Lot was told. "Escape to the mountain, lest thou be consumed."

Lot's wife could not break off her ties with the past. Her previous life was dead, but she could not admit it. So, disobeying the Lord's command, she turned and looked at the splendid, sinful city that lay behind her. And as she looked, the Lord rained fire and brimstone upon it.

Near the south end of the Dead Sea, on Mount Sodom, for centuries the natives have pointed to a pillar of rock salt.

"Lot's wife," they say.

71

Jochebed

Mothers may do foolish things, but one kind of wisdom is bred in their bones—the wisdom they need to protect their babies. Even animal mothers have it. The doe with a new fawn, seeing a wildcat creeping up, will make a noise and draw the marauder off in pursuit, leaving her baby safely hidden in a thicket.

Jochebed was a loving mother and a wise one. Her people, the Israelites, dwelled in Egypt. The tribes had grown in numbers, and Pharaoh felt they were becoming a threat to his people. So he commanded that every newborn Hebrew boy should be put to death.

Jochebed already had one child, a daughter, Miriam, when she gave birth to a son. For three months she hid the boy, but then he was too big to conceal. With careful, anxious hands she wove a stout little ark of bulrushes and smeared it with pitch to make it watertight. Then, laying her son in the ark, she carried it to the edge of the Nile and set it amid the reeds, so it would not float away. She left Miriam to watch at a distance, and she herself went away. But not very far away.

After a time, Miriam saw a flurry of activity at the water's edge. The daughter of Pharaoh had come to bathe in the Nile. We can suspect that the princess came there regularly and that it was not purely by chance Jochebed had chosen that particular spot to leave her son.

The princess's curiosity was aroused by the little ark floating in the water. Soon the baby, crying, was in her arms. She knew at once he was a Hebrew child and she felt great compassion for him.

Suddenly there was a young girl at the side of the princess. "Shall I go and call to thee a nurse of the Hebrew women, that she may nurse the child for thee?" she asked.

"Go," the princess commanded.

Miriam raced off and brought back her mother.

And so, that very day, the infant Moses was suckling happily at his mother's breast again. He was secure from harm, under the protection of a mighty princess, who loved him as though he were her own son.

That little baby was to become the greatest leader in Hebrew history. Later, when the children of Israel dreamed of the coming of the Messiah, they used to say, "He will be one like Moses."

Great leaders have great mothers. Jesus had Mary. Moses had Jochebed.

The Queen of Sheba I KINGS 10:1-13

Over nine hundred years before the birth of our Lord, a great caravan set forth on a journey from Saba, or Sheba, in southern Arabia. Golden bells tinkled on richly caparisoned camels as mounted warriors with burnished weapons galloped up and down the line. For the caravan carried not only a rich treasure in gold, precious stones, and spices, but the queen of Sheba herself.

The queen—the Arabs say her name was Balkis—had heard of the wisdom of Solomon, king of Israel, and she was coming, the Bible tells us, "to prove him with hard questions." It was a lengthy journey, some twelve hundred miles, and queens did not ordinarily travel such great distances, but the reigning monarch of Sheba was no ordinary queen.

The queen had a boundless curiosity and an insatiable love of knowledge. "She was inquisitive unto philosophy, and on other accounts also was to be admired," the historian Flavius Josephus declares. One reason for which we can admire her is that she did not believe in relying on second-hand reports. She had to see for herself.

73

The queen of Sheba wanted to learn all she could from Solomon because she wished to advance the prosperity of her own country. He had mines of copper and iron, and ships that plied up and down the seas, bringing gold and silver, ivory, and apes, and peacocks from far away. Israel enjoyed a golden age while Solomon sat upon the throne. And so "the queen of the South," in the words of Jesus (Matthew 12:42), "came from the uttermost parts of the earth to hear the wisdom of Solomon."

The queen tested Solomon with her questions, and in his replies the king held nothing back from her. Finally she said to him, "It was a true report that I heard in mine own land of thy acts and of thy wisdom. Howbeit I believed not the words, until I came, and mine eyes had seen it: and, behold, the half was not told me: thy wisdom and prosperity exceedeth the fame which I heard."

As a token of her appreciation, the queen gave Solomon glorious presents. Among them was a gift of 120 gold talents—several million dollars by today's standard. And Solomon in turn gave her whatever she desired. Thus these two wise monarchs cemented a strong bond of friendship between their two countries.

According to legend, the queen and Solomon had a romance. The Old Testament does not mention it and relates only that the queen and her servants went back to their own country at the end of the visit. However, the royal family of Ethiopia traces its descent from Menelik I, who, tradition says, was the son of Solomon and the queen of Sheba.

Huldah II KINGS 22: 14-20

Where prophesy is concerned, women for the most part had little to say in the Bible. But Huldah is an exception to this circumstance and is unusual both as an example of a woman acting as a prophet and for her insight and ability with respect to the fulfilment of prophesy.

Huldah was the wife of Shallum, "keeper of the wardrobe" We know that information and gossip is often available in such a situation. Perhaps that is why she was the one consulted when King Josiah sent to "inquire of the Lord" after finding the Book of the Law in the temple. She prophesied God's judgement upon the nation, but peace for Josiah because of his repentance.

After consultation with Huldah, King Josiah carried out his religious reforms (II Kings 23: 1-25). "And like unto him was there no king before him, that turned to the Lord with all his heart, and with all his soul, and with all his might, according to the law of Moses; neither after him arose there any like him."

Not only was Huldah's prophesy effective for initiating drastic reform and improvements, but it was completely fulfilled when Josiah found peace with God before he was later killed at Megiddo warring against the king of Assyria.

Quite a remarkable record for the wife of a wardrobe keeper and even more so for the perception and wisdom shown by one of the humble women in the Bible.

The Chaste and
the Unchaste

Who can find a virtuous woman? for her price is far above rubies.
The heart of her husband doth safely trust in her, so that he shall
have no need of spoil. Proverbs 31:10-11

Neither shalt thou commit adultery. Deuteronomy 5:18

Walk in the Spirit, and ye shall not fulfill the lust of the flesh.
Galatians 5:16

Women were expected to live up to a strict standard in Old Testament times. The first requirement was that a woman should be virtuous. "A virtuous woman is a crown to her husband." (Proverbs 12:4)

A man's name lived on through his children, and only if his wife was faithful could he be sure they were his children. Women like Sarah and Ruth personify virtue in womanhood, just as Potiphar's wife stands for wickedness. In the New Testament, Mary, the Holy Mother, represents all that is good and noble in woman.

As much as the chaste woman was praised, the unchaste woman was condemned. Men were warned to stay away from her. No matter how attractive she might be, no good could come of associating with her. "For the lips of a strange woman drop as an honeycomb, and her mouth is smoother than oil: But her end is as bitter as wormwood, sharp as a twoedged sword" (Proverbs 5:3,4). "But whoso committeth adultery with a woman lacketh understanding: he that doeth it destroyeth his own soul" (Proverbs 6:32).

Punishment for a person taken in adultery was severe under the code of Moses. The guilty party was put to death.

The coming of Christ brought a new dispensation for sinners. Jesus did not shun harlots or adulteresses, but held out the hand of redemption to them. This does not mean that He sanctioned

77

their sins. Far from it. He admitted them to His kingdom only if they repented.

Bathsheba
II SAMUEL 11:2-17; 12:24; I KINGS 1:11-31; 2:13-24; I CHRONICLES 3:5; MATTHEW 1:6

Was Bathsheba an adulteress? She did take part in an act of adultery, but she did not do so of her own free will or wish. In old Palestine, when a king commanded a woman to submit to him, she could not refuse and still go on living.

Bathsheba was a remarkable beauty. One evening as she was washing herself on the roof of her husband's house, King David, looking down from the roof of his palace nearby, saw her and wanted her. For David, the next step was to have her. He sent soldiers to her house. They did not ask her if she wanted to go; they simply took her. Later they brought her home. Her husband, Uriah the Hittite, was away, fighting at the front.

How Bathsheba felt about her strange experience the Old Testament does not tell. Perhaps she was pledged, on pain of death, not to reveal anything to her husband. But when she became pregnant she knew she could not keep her secret for long. "I am with child," she said in an urgent message to David.

One of the greatest biblical heroes, David was also one of the greatest sinners. A scandal had to be avoided, he decided; Uriah had to be convinced the child that Bathsheba was bearing was his. But Uriah had been away with the army for months. The only possible solution, it seemed to the king, was get him home immediately.

All at once Uriah found himself ordered back to Jerusalem. He was told to report directly to the king about the conduct of the war. David pretended to listen with interest to what Uriah had to say, but he could not wait for him to finish. "Go down to thy house, and wash thy feet," the king urged. Actually, he was hinting that Uriah should spend some time with his wife.

Surprisingly, Uriah spent the night at the palace. When the king, swallowing his anger, asked the warrior why he had not gone home, Uriah reminded him that his fellow soldiers were bivouacking in the open fields. "Shall I then go into mine house, to eat and to drink, and to lie with my wife? as thou livest, and as thy soul liveth, I will not do this thing."

The king was not ready to give up. Perhaps drink would weaken Uriah's conscience. But the warrior, although reeling, still could not forget his comrades in the war. Again he chose to sleep in the palace.

David was not a patient man. He had given Uriah two chances to be with his wife and he had refused them. Almost at once Uriah was ordered back to the front. In his hand he carried a sealed message to the commanding general: "Set ye Uriah in the forefront of the hottest battle, and retire ye from him, that he may be smitten and die."

An order is an order; Uriah fell in battle and never learned of his wife's dishonor. Bathsheba mourned for her slain husband, while David counted the days. When her period of mourning was at an end David made her his wife.

Bathsheba gave birth to a son, but he was not destined to bring joy to her. The Lord knew why Uriah had died and he was angry. So he sent the prophet Nathan to the king to remind him of his sin and to tell him the baby would die. Although David fasted and prayed, the Lord refused to take pity on him. For Bathsheba the loss of her firstborn must have been intensely painful.

But happier days lay ahead for David's new wife. The first legitimate child she bore the king was Solomon. Later she had three more children.

When David was old, Bathsheba persuaded him to name Solomon as his successor. It was a wise choice; under him Israel enjoyed a golden age. A king, Solomon gave his mother a place of honor close to his throne. What he thought of her is shown in his reply when she told him she had a request to make. "Ask on, my mother: for I will not say thee nay."

Bathsheba had sinned when she was a young woman, but she had expiated, and God gave her a long and rewarding life. She had many descendants, including Joseph, the husband of Mary.

Sarah GENESIS 11:29-31; 12:5, 11-20; 13-1; 16:1-16;
17:15-21; 18:1-15; 20:2-18; 21:1-12; 23:1, 2,
19; 24:36, 67; 25:10, 12; 49:31

Sarah (her name, at first, was Sarai) was the wife of the patriarch
Abraham. A virtuous and a loving woman, she followed her husband unhesitatingly wherever he went, sharing his life of wander-
ing and tribulation.

Famine was a constant threat in Bible times. It drove Abraham
and his wife into Egypt in search of food. As they approached the
border, Abraham looked apprehensively at his wife. She was
beautiful, and many men had desired her. Now he feared the
Egyptians would take her from him, and they would kill him if
they knew he was her husband. So he asked his wife to pretend
to be his sister. (She was, in fact, his half-sister.) That way he
might be spared.

When the princes of Egypt beheld Sarah they admired her;
soon she was being ushered into Pharaoh's harem. Pharaoh,
believing Abraham was her brother, gave him many presents.
But the Lord meant to keep Sarah for her rightful husband, and
he struck Pharaoh and his house with great plagues. Finally
Pharaoh, grasping God's intent, sent Sarah and Abraham out of
his land. She was happy to have her husband back; the Egyptian
sovereign and his treasures meant nothing to her.

Years later the patriarch's travels took him into Gerar. The
king, Abimelech, cast adoring glances at Sarah. Again Abraham
said she was his sister, and Abimelech took her into his harem. In
retribution, the Lord closed the wombs of the women in the king's
family. As soon as Abimelech set Sarah free, God lifted his curse.

The Lord had prophesied that Sarah would bear a son, but as
the years slipped by she despaired. At length she gave her hand-
maiden, Hagar, to Abraham, to be his wife. Hagar only made
trouble for Sarah and in the end Sarah turned her out. (Hagar's
story is told earlier in this book.)

After many years, Sarah did conceive. She was already an old
woman when she bore Isaac. She could hardly believe in her good

fortune. "Who would have said unto Abraham," she declared, "that Sarah would have given children suck? for I have born him a son in his old age." It was the first case of a miraculous birth in the Bible.

Sarah lived a happy and useful life, dying at a great age. Her husband buried her in the Cave of Machpelah, where his bones were later to be laid. You can still see her tomb there today.

To the early Christians, Sarah was a woman of special importance. "Through faith," said the apostle Paul, "also Sarah herself received strength to conceive seed, and was delivered of a child when she was past age, because she judged him faithful who had promised" (Hebrews 11:11).

The Sinful Woman LUKE 7:36-50

Once Jesus accepted the invitation of Simon the Pharisee to eat at his house. As Jesus sat at the table, a woman who was a sinner came in. She stood behind the Master, tears streaming down her face. Then, with her tears, she began to wash His feet. Drying them with her long hair, she kissed them and anointed them with ointment from an alabaster box she had brought.

Simon was shocked that the Master did not thrust the woman away. The Pharisee told himself that if He were a true prophet, He would surely have known she was a sinner.

"Simon," said Jesus, for He could read the Pharisee's mind "I have somewhat to say unto thee." And He told him a parable of two debtors. One owed five hundred pence and the other owed fifty, but neither could pay. Their creditor, however, generously forgave them. "Tell me therefore," Jesus asked, "which of them will love him most?"

81

"He to whom he forgave most."

"Thou hast judged rightly," Jesus said. And He told Simon that the woman, by her actions, had demonstrated that she loved Jesus much more than Simon did. "Her sins, which are many, are forgiven." Jesus turned to the woman. "Thy faith hath saved thee," he said. "Go in peace."

Jacob had twelve sons, but of them all Joseph was his favorite. Joseph's brothers were extremely jealous of him, especially after their father made him a coat of many colors. At first the brothers plotted to kill him, but then they decided they could rid themselves of him just as effectively by selling him into slavery. A band of Ishmaelites bought him and took him with them to Egypt. There he was sold to Potiphar, captain of Pharaoh's guard and a man of considerable importance.

The Hebrew slave soon proved his worth to his master. Potiphar advanced the youth to be overseer over all his possessions. It was a wise move for Potiphar prospered more than ever.

The new overseer was a handsome young man, a fact that did not escape the restless eyes of Potiphar's unfaithful wife. When her husband was away, she tried to tempt Joseph to make love to her. Joseph was shocked. He reminded his mistress that Potiphar placed complete trust in him. "How then can I do this great wickedness and sin against God?" he said.

Although Joseph feared God, Potiphar's wife did not. Once she had set her mind on something, she did not give up easily. Another time, as Joseph was walking by, she reached out and caught him by his garment. "Lie with me," she whispered. Joseph pulled away so vigorously he left the garment in her hand.

Potiphar's wife was not used to being refused. Her heart turned black with spite. Suddenly she saw how she could take revenge on Joseph. Carrying the garment to her husband, she told him his overseer had tried to attack her. "And it came to pass," she said, "as I lifted up my voice and cried, that he left his garment with me, and fled out."

Potiphar, in spite of his high position, must have been a very gullible man; his wife could tell him anything and he would believe her. Rape or attempted rape was a serious crime, and the young Hebrew was thrown into prison, but even within the thick stone walls the Lord was with Joseph. The warden recognized that he possessed remarkable talents, and placed him over the other prisoners. He won a reputation as an interpreter of dreams and before very long he was released to demonstrate his skill to Pharaoh himself.

After she denounced Joseph to her husband, Potiphar's wife disappears from the pages of the Old Testament. Through her infidelity and double-dealing she had done enough to win a place for herself in the memory of mankind. Just as Jezebel stands as a symbol of the wicked, shameless woman, Potiphar's wife symbolizes the woman who betrays her husband.

Dinah GENESIS 30:21; 34:1-31; 46:15

Dinah was the daughter of Leah and Jacob. When her father stopped for a while in the land of Shalem, she went out to see its women. Before she came home again her life had been changed forever.

As Dinah walked through the countryside a man saw her and coveted her. His name was Shechem, and he was the son of Hamor, prince of the country. Shechem "took her, and lay with her, and defiled her." The words of the Bible make it clear that Dinah did not encourage him but was taken by force.

Now Shechem found he had a special feeling for Dinah: he loved her. "Get me this damsel to wife," he said to his father, Hamor.

Hamor and Shechem met with Jacob and his sons and tried to ingratiate themselves, for they knew Shechem had done wrong. Hamor even invited the Hebrews to settle in his land and intermarry with his people. "Let me find grace in your eyes, and what ye shall say unto me I will give."

Even so, Jacob's sons raised an objection to the marriage of Dinah and Shechem for they could not allow their sister to wed a man who was uncircumcised. However, if all the males of the city would consent to be circumcised, they said, they would give Dinah to Shechem and remain in Shalem. The prince and his son accepted the proposal, and they persuaded all the men of the city to undergo the rite of circumcision.

But Simeon and Levi, two of Jacob's sons, had not forgiven Shechem for what he had done to their sister, in spite of his willingness to make amends. On the third day they went and killed him and his father. Then they fell upon all the rest of the men in the city and slew them, too. They seized all the possessions of the dead Shalemites as well as their wives and children.

When Jacob heard what his hotheaded sons had done he was horrified. He was in an alien land, and he could well imagine how its inhabitants would take the slayings. "They shall gather themselves together against me, and slay me; and I shall be destroyed, I and my house."

But Simon and Levi refused to admit they had done wrong. They were still furious with Shechem as they answered their father: "Should he deal with our sister as with an harlot?"

Gomer HOSEA 1:3

Gomer is a strange figure, one of the strangest in the Old Testament. It is difficult to tell whether she is a woman of flesh and blood or a purely allegorical figure. Possibly she is both.

In the Book of Hosea, Gomer is the wife of the prophet Hosea. Hosea, who lived in Israel in the time of Jeroboam II, over seven hundred years before Christ, was highly regarded by later generations; his book is quoted many times in the New Testament. He married Gomer, he tells us, in response to a command from the Lord: "Go, take unto thee a wife of whoredoms and children of whoredoms: for the land hath committed great whoredom, departing from the Lord."

Gomer was repeatedly unfaithful to her husband. She bore several children who were not Hosea's, and she deserted him. Still, he loved her; he sought her out and took her back. "Thou shalt abide for me many days," he told her. "Thou shalt not play the harlot, and thou shalt not be for another man: so will I also be for thee."

In Hosea's allegory, Gomer is more than a woman. She is the

land of Israel, which had turned away from the Lord and worshiped Baal. But God, like Hosea, loved her, and was ready to forgive her sins and welcome her back into his arms.

Tamar GENESIS 38:6-30

Tamar was the daughter-in-law of Judah, one of the brothers of Joseph, who was sold into bondage in Egypt. Her story seems curious to us today because it reflects the customs of another age, but it does show us how important motherhood was to Hebrew women in Old Testament days.

Tamar was married to Er, Judah's firstborn son, but Er was wicked and the Lord slew him. In keeping with the custom, Tamar was next married to Er's brother, Onan. Onan was unwilling to have children, and God took his life, too.

Judah still had another son, Shelah, then still a boy; he told Tamar he would give her to him when he was grown. But Judah did not keep his promise, for he feared Shelah might meet the same fate as his brothers.

Hearing that Judah would be passing by, Tamar put off her widow's garments. She dressed herself as a harlot, covered her face with a veil, and sat by the roadside. Finally Judah came by. He failed to recognize his daughter-in-law and went into her tent. As a pledge that he would pay for her services he gave Tamar his bracelets, his signets, and his staff. But when he sent the payment Tamar could not be found.

Later Judah heard his daughter-in-law had become pregnant out of wedlock. Tradition required that she should be put to death. Before anything could be done to her, Tamar showed Judah's staff, signets, and bracelets. He was astounded. "She hath been more righteous than I," he said, admitting he should have given her to his son, Shelah.

Although Tamar played the harlot, she was not really one. She was merely enforcing her right to have children under the Jewish law. King David was a descendant of one of the twin sons she bore nine months after Judah had come to her tent.

85

The Woman Taken in Adultery

As Jesus was teaching in the temple the scribes and Pharisees brought a woman to him. This woman, they told Him, had been taken in adultery, and the law said she should be put to death. "But what sayest thou?" they asked. They hoped He would contradict the law and they could bring charges against Him.

Jesus did not answer them. He stooped and wrote in the dust, pretending not to hear the men. But they kept questioning Him.

Finally He answered them. His quiet words had the sharp points of spears. "He that is without sin among you, let him first cast a stone at her."

Struck with shame, the accusers could not reply. One by one they slunk away.

Jesus was left alone with the woman. He looked at her.

"Hath no man condemned thee?" He asked.

"No man, Lord."

"Neither do I condemn thee: go, and sin no more."

The Master had given the adulteress a second chance. It was a blessed moment for the woman—a single miraculous moment when the path was suddenly opened to her to walk from darkness into a life of light.

Other Women in the Bible

Space does not permit detailed accounts of every woman in the Bible. Names of all those not described are given in the list below for further reference and investigation.

Abi	Cozbi	Joanna	Prisca
Abiah	Damaris	Judah	Puah
Abihail	Drusilla	Judith	Reumah
Abijah	Eglah	Julia	Rhoda
Abishag	Elisheba	Keren-happuch	Serah
Abital	Ephah	Keturah	Shelomith
Achsah	Ephratah	Kezia	Sherah
Adah	Ephrath	Lo-ruhamah	Shimeath
Agar	Euodias	Maacah	Shimrith
Ahinoam	Hadassah	Maachah	Shiphrah
Ahlai	Haggith	Mahalah	Shomer
Aholah	Hammoleketh	Mahalath	Shua
Aholibah	Hamutal	Mahlah	Susanna
Aholibamah	Hazelelponi	Mara	Syntyche
Anah	Helah	Matred	Tahpenes
Apphia	Heph-zibah	Mehetabel	Taphath
Asenath	Hodesh	Merab	Thamar
Atarah	Hodiah	Meshullemeth	Timna
Azubah	Hoglah	Michaiah	Tirzah
Baara	Hushim	Milcah	Tryphena
Bashemath	Iscah	Naamah	Tryphosa
Basmath	Jecholiah	Naarah	Zebudah
Bath-shua	Jedidah	Nehushta	Zeresh
Bernice	Jehoaddan	Noadiah	Zeruah
Bilhah	Jehosheba	Noah	Zeruiah
Bithiah	Jehudijah	Oholibamah	Zibiah
Candace	Jemima	Peninnah	Zillah
Chloe	Jerioth	Persis	Zilpah
Claudia	Jerusha	Phanuel	Zipporah

Yet hear the word of the Lord,
                    O ye women — Jeremiah 9:20

That our sons may be as plants grown up in their youth; that our daughters may be as corner stones, polished after the similitude of a palace . . . Happy is that people, that is in such a case; yea, happy is that people, whose God is the Lord. Psalm 144: 12, 15

Favour is deceitful, and beauty is vain: but a woman that feareth the Lord, she shall be praised. Give her of the fruit of her hands; and let her own works praise her in the gates. Proverbs 31: 30, 31

Therefore, my brethren dearly beloved and longed for, my joy and crown, so stand fast in the Lord, my dearly beloved. And I intreat thee also, true yokefellow, help those women which laboured with me in the gospel, . . whose names are in the book of life. Philippians 4:1, 3